AT A GLANCE

Essential Court Tables for Ancillary Relief

Produced for The FLBA by
CLASS PUBLISHING • LONDON

Copyright © The Family Law Bar Association 1992, 1993
All rights reserved

First annual edition published 1992, reprinted 1992
Second annual edition published 1993

A CIP catalogue record for this book is available from the
British Library

ISBN 1 872362 18 4

Further copies of this book and future editions
may be ordered from

The Publications Secretary
The Family Law Bar Association
1 Mitre Court Buildings
Temple
London EC4Y 7BS

Telephone 071 797 7070
Fax 071 797 7435

Produced for The FLBA by
Class Publishing
PO Box 1498
London W6 7RS

Cover design by Wendy Bann
Edited by Susan Bosanko

Printed by
Cheney & Sons Ltd
Beaumont Road
Banbury
Oxon OX16 7RH

Foreword to the 1993 Edition

by

The President of the Family Division
The Rt. Hon. Sir Stephen Brown

I am delighted to have the opportunity of commending a new Edition of this valuable work. *At a Glance* has proved to be of great assistance to judges and practitioners alike.

The updated and the additional Tables convey information with admirable clarity whilst the expanded selection of Leading Cases comprises an excellent point of departure for virtually every category of financial application. Indeed for many, if not most, there will be no need to look further.

I would not be without it*!*

Preface 1993-94

The story thus far . . .

Gentle readers will recall the tribulations, but not yet the trial, foreshadowed by the first edition's masterly preface:

> 'After the Act V reconciliation of the Montagues with the Capulets outside the funerary vault, Romeo and Juliet emerge unscathed and reveal the lengths to which they have gone to bring their families to their senses. A large dowry is bestowed which Romeo rapidly realises, investing the proceeds of the Index-linked National Savings Certificates, the share portfolio and the Palladian villa in his newly-formed balcony construction company.
>
> Several years and a pair of twins later passion-spent Romeo abandons Verona and his responsibilities for the rival attractions of Rome and a rich widow. For the moment Juliet will only want to know what are her and the children's State Benefits. But once she realises Romeo has departed from her stage for ever, she sets the scene for financial retribution.
>
> What lump sum including capitalised maintenance may she expect, bearing in mind the value her dowry would now have and thus her contributions? Has sufficient consideration been given to her transport costs? As Romeo is no longer within the jurisdiction of Verona, should she seek a lump sum to secure the expense of the twins' schooling? Why should she not seek recompense for the potential loss of widow's pension rights?
>
> Romeo for his part is anxious to demonstrate how tax has historically eroded his income and how the real cost of school fees has risen year by year. Now he is paid in lire he suggests the exchange rate with the ducat will benefit Juliet (if past trends are any guide). He asserts her income capacity is considerable, even after tax. He points out that his shareholdings are pregnant with capital gains so that his real wealth is less than would at first sight appear . . .'

But now a year on . . .

and still the hearing date for the ancillary relief case has not been fixed – they may well need a perpetual calendar to write it on. The only consolation is the appearance of the new edition of *At a Glance*, with all its original materials updated, and so much more besides.

Juliet can check her and the twins' entitlement by reference to the new Income Support and the other Social Security Tables, though she will need a rather weightier tome to master the plethora of state benefit detail. Hopefully her advisers have shrewdly invested in a copy of *Child's Pay* with which to comprehend if not indeed to master the Machiavellian intricacies of the Child Support Act.

And now Romeo can at least compare the cost of living in Rome as against Verona to see if that will aid his cause. And Juliet has a way of estimating, in broad terms, the value of that Balcony Gazebo and Conservatory (he has diversified) Construction Company.

Detailed consideration of the scale and comparative real worth of awards in previous big-money cases gives her hope, and causes him despair. How much, he wonders, would he have to earn gross to satisfy her maintenance demands if he cannot secure the clean break he so much craves?

A serious cause for deliberation is the **Duxbury** table. Were the editors right to stick to actuarial table PA90 as the basis for the life expectancy element of the calculation, given that (as the notes to table 17 explain) the mortality table ELT14, taken from statistics for the population as a whole, suggests a shorter life expectancy and thus a **Duxbury** figure between about 2% and 8% lower than PA90 produces and table 18 displays? Or is the answer that once Juliet receives her capitalised maintenance she will become as healthy and stress-free as the pensioners in insured pension schemes whose statistics contribute to PA90, and who to be sure they exhaust their fund thus live those few years longer?

The answers, if not in the Tables, are sure to be in the Leading Cases, and failing all else in the words of the key sections of the 1973 Act itself.

Contents

Acknowledgements

The Family Law Bar Association acknowledges with thanks the assistance it has received from the following companies and organisations which have agreed to material derived from them being incorporated in this volume:

The Automobile Association
The Bank of England
The Central Statistical Office
Coopers & Lybrand
The Economist
The Equitable Life
Ernst & Young
Family Law

The Financial Times
The Halifax Building Society
Her Majesty's Stationery Office
The Independent Schools Information Service
The National Foster Care Association
Peter Lobbenberg & Co
Royal Life
Savings Certificate and SAYE Office

The Family Law Bar Association thanks the Editorial Committee responsible for the production of this volume:

The Hon. Mr Justice Singer
James Holman QC
Valentine Le Grice
Nicholas Mostyn
Gavin Smith
Katharine Davidson
Timothy Bishop

Although care has been taken to ensure the reliability of the contents of this volume neither The Family Law Bar Association nor any of its officers or members warrants their accuracy.

The Family Law Bar Association publishes *At a Glance* annually, incorporating fresh and up-dated material. The Editorial Committee would welcome suggestions, whether for the improvement of existing or for the addition of further tables.

Tables 6, 11 (part), 15 (part), 18, 21, 26, 27 and Leading Cases are the copyright of Nicholas Mostyn and must not be reproduced without his permission. He has asserted his rights in accordance with the Copyright, Designs and Patents Act 1988.

The Perpetual Calendar is taken from the *Collins Management Diary*, published by the Stationery and Diary Division of HarperCollins Publishers and is reproduced with their permission.

Table 1   Retail Price Index

	1954	1955	1956	1957	1958	1959	1960	1961	1962	1963
Jan	10.27	10.70	11.25	11.74	12.17	12.42	12.37	12.62	13.21	13.56
Feb	10.27	10.70	11.25	11.74	12.09	12.40	12.37	12.62	13.23	13.69
Mar	10.34	10.70	11.38	11.71	12.19	12.40	12.34	12.67	13.28	13.71
Apr	10.42	10.77	11.56	11.76	12.32	12.32	12.40	12.75	13.46	13.74
May	10.34	10.77	11.53	11.76	12.29	12.27	12.40	12.78	13.51	13.74
Jun	10.42	11.00	11.51	11.89	12.40	12.29	12.47	12.90	13.59	13.74
Jul	10.62	11.00	11.48	11.99	12.19	12.40	12.50	12.90	13.54	13.66
Aug	10.57	10.93	11.51	11.96	12.19	12.29	12.42	13.00	13.43	13.61
Sep	10.49	11.00	11.48	11.94	12.19	12.22	12.42	13.00	13.41	13.66
Oct	10.57	11.15	11.56	12.04	12.29	12.29	12.52	13.00	13.41	13.71
Nov	10.62	11.28	11.58	12.12	12.34	12.37	12.60	13.16	12.46	13.74
Dec	10.62	11.28	11.63	12.17	12.40	12.40	12.62	13.18	13.51	13.76

	1964	1965	1966	1967	1968	1969	1970	1971	1972	1973
Jan	13.84	14.47	15.11	15.67	16.07	17.06	17.90	19.42	21.01	22.64
Feb	13.84	14.47	15.11	15.67	16.15	17.16	18.00	19.54	21.12	22.79
Mar	13.89	14.52	15.13	15.67	16.20	17.21	18.10	19.70	21.19	22.92
Apr	14.02	14.80	15.34	15.79	16.50	17.41	18.38	20.13	21.39	23.35
May	14.14	14.85	15.44	15.79	16.50	17.39	18.43	20.25	21.50	23.52
Jun	14.20	14.90	15.49	15.84	16.58	17.47	18.48	20.38	21.62	23.65
Jul	14.20	14.90	15.41	15.74	16.58	17.47	18.63	20.51	21.70	23.75
Aug	14.25	14.93	15.51	15.72	16.60	17.41	18.61	20.53	21.88	23.83
Sep	14.25	14.93	15.49	15.69	16.63	17.47	18.71	20.56	22.00	24.03
Oct	14.27	14.96	15.51	15.82	16.70	17.59	18.91	20.66	22.31	24.51
Nov	14.37	15.01	15.61	15.92	16.76	17.64	19.04	20.79	22.38	24.69
Dec	14.42	15.08	15.64	16.02	16.96	17.77	19.16	20.89	22.48	24.87

	1974	1975	1976	1977	1978	1979	1980	1981	1982	1983
Jan	25.35	30.39	37.49	43.70	48.03	52.52	62.18	70.29	78.73	82.61
Feb	25.78	30.90	37.97	44.13	48.31	52.95	63.07	70.93	78.76	82.97
Mar	26.00	31.51	38.17	44.56	48.62	53.38	63.93	71.99	79.44	83.12
Apr	26.89	32.72	38.91	45.70	49.33	54.30	66.11	74.07	81.04	84.28
May	27.28	34.09	39.34	46.06	49.61	54.73	66.72	74.55	81.62	84.64
Jun	27.55	34.75	39.54	46.54	49.99	55.67	67.35	74.98	81.85	84.84
Jul	27.81	35.11	39.62	46.59	50.22	58.07	67.91	75.31	81.88	85.30
Aug	27.83	35.31	40.18	46.82	50.54	58.53	68.06	75.87	81.90	85.68
Sep	28.14	35.61	40.71	47.07	50.75	59.11	68.49	76.30	81.85	86.06
Oct	28.69	36.12	41.44	47.28	50.98	59.72	68.92	76.98	82.26	86.36
Nov	29.20	36.55	42.03	47.50	51.33	60.25	69.48	77.79	82.66	86.67
Dec	29.63	37.01	42.59	47.76	51.76	60.68	69.86	78.28	82.51	86.89

	1984	1985	1986	1987	1988	1989	1990	1991	1992	1993
Jan	86.84	91.20	96.25	100.00	103.30	111.00	119.50	130.25	135.60	137.90
Feb	87.20	91.94	96.60	100.40	103.70	111.80	120.22	130.97	136.30	138.70
Mar	87.48	92.80	96.73	100.60	104.10	112.30	121.41	131.44	136.70	139.30
Apr	88.64	94.78	97.67	101.80	105.80	114.30	125.15	133.14	138.80	
May	88.97	95.21	97.85	101.90	106.20	115.00	126.25	133.56	139.30	
Jun	89.20	95.41	97.79	101.90	106.60	115.40	126.76	134.15	139.30	
Jul	89.10	95.23	97.52	101.80	106.70	115.50	126.85	133.80	138.80	
Aug	89.94	95.49	97.82	102.10	107.90	115.80	128.12	134.10	138.90	
Sep	90.11	95.44	98.30	102.40	108.40	116.60	129.31	134.60	139.40	
Oct	90.67	95.59	98.45	102.90	109.50	117.50	130.33	135.10	139.90	
Nov	90.95	95.92	99.29	103.40	110.00	118.50	129.99	135.60	139.70	
Dec	90.87	96.05	99.62	103.30	110.30	118.80	129.91	135.70	139.20	

Further information

More detailed information may be obtained from the *Employment Gazette* Tables 6.1-6.8; and the Central Statistical Office *Monthly Digest of Statistics* Tables 18.1-18.3; or by telephoning the recorded message on 0923 800511 (6 lines).

How to calculate the effect of inflation

from one month to any subsequent month

The formula is **X × A ÷ B**

Where **X** is the figure to be inflated
   A is the RPI for the later month
   B is the RPI for the earlier month
   (e.g. when asset acquired or previous order made)

Table 2   Financial Times Index

Level of the FT All-Share Index at month-end for the past 10 years

Year	Jan	Feb	Mar	Apr	May	Jun	Jul	Aug	Sep	Oct	Nov	Dec
83	395.02	399.35	411.94	439.29	437.63	458.91	445.91	450.36	445.53	437.38	461.87	470.50
84	501.36	493.12	542.20	534.83	477.21	487.74	474.83	520.47	535.86	543.48	560.26	592.94
85	614.62	508.28	616.26	622.11	634.16	595.54	603.46	646.26	626.24	670.64	696.53	682.94
86	696.41	750.83	810.48	816.40	788.92	815.70	771.80	817.06	768.79	807.27	815.34	835.48
87	903.29	983.12	1,000.04	1,023.58	1,097.29	1,153.12	1,202.19	1,146.69	1,208.89	887.33	796.31	870.22
88	915.84	908.08	896.75	928.19	923.52	963.01	965.18	911.17	946.27	965.54	933.45	926.59
89	1,054.97	1,042.60	1,076.15	1,090.04	1,091.06	1,101.67	1,173.25	1,207.45	1,169.55	1,080.79	1,138.67	1,204.70
90	1,167.15	1,122.26	1,114.94	1,043.16	1,154.24	1,171.28	1,147.05	1,051.08	962.18	992.67	1,032.11	1,032.25
91	1,036.24	1,150.01	1,193.33	1,202.75	1,201.85	1,161.19	1,235.89	1,268.62	1,265.96	1,238.63	1,168.95	1,187.70
92	1,227.63	1,229,84	1,171.71	1,282.75	1,311.79	1,216.62	1,143.14	1,096.99	1,206.16	1,256.67	1,313.02	1,363.79
93	1,364.33	1,396.53	1,408.07	1,388.88								

Table 3   Judgment Debt Interest Rates

Pursuant to s 17 Judgments Act 1838

	Date	%
Before	20 April 1971	4.00
Since	20 April 1971	7.50
	1 March 1977	10.00
	3 December 1979	12.50
	9 June 1980	15.00
	8 June 1982	14.00
	10 November 1982	12.00
	16 April 1985	15.00
	1 April 1993	8.00

Table 4   Interest Base Rates

This table shows the dates of change in the base rate of the four largest London Clearing Banks (Barclays, Lloyds, Midland and National Westminster) at close of business on the respective days

Date	New rate (%)	Date	New rate (%)	Date	New rate (%)
1980		20 August	10.50	11 April	8.00
4 July	16.00	7 November	10.00	18 May	7.50
25 November	14.00	20 November	9.875*	3 June	8.00
		23 November	9.625*	6 June	8.25*
1981				7 June	8.50
11 March	12.00	**1985**		22 June	9.00
16 September	14.00	11 January	10.50	29 June	9.50
1 October	16.00	14 January	12.00	5 July	10.00
14 October	15.50	28 January	14.00	19 July	10.50
9 November	15.00	20 March	13.75*	8 August	10.75*
3 December	14.50	21 March	13.50	9 August	11.00
		29 March	13.25*	25 August	11.50*
1982		2 April	13.125*	26 August	12.00
12 January	14.00	12 April	12.875*	25 November	13.00
25 February	13.50	19 April	12.675*		
12 March	13.00	12 June	12.50	**1989**	
8 June	12.50	7 July	12.25*	24 May	14.00
13 July	12.00	16 July	12.00	5 October	15.00
2 August	11.50	29 July	11.75*		
18 August	11.00	30 July	11.50	**1990**	
31 August	10.50			8 October	14.00
7 October	10.00	**1986**			
14 October	9.50	9 January	12.50	**1991**	
4 November	9.00	19 March	11.50	13 February	13.50
26 November	10.125*	8 April	11.25*	27 February	13.00
		9 April	11.00	25 March	12.50
1983		24 April	10.50	12 April	12.00
12 January	11.00	27 May	10.00	24 May	11.50
15 March	10.50	14 October	11.00	12 July	11.00
15 April	10.00			4 September	10.50
15 June	9.50	**1987**			
4 October	9.00	10 March	10.50	**1992**	
		19 March	10.00	5 May	10.00
1984		29 April	9.50	16 September	12.00
7 March	8.875*	11 May	9.00	17 September	10.00
15 March	8.625*	7 August	10.00	22 September	9.00
10 May	9.125*	26 October	9.50	16 October	8.00
27 June	9.25	5 November	9.00	13 November	7.00
9 July	10.00	4 December	8.50		
11 July	11.00*			**1993**	
12 July	12.00	**1988**		26 January	6.00
9 August	11.50	2 February	9.00		
10 August	11.00	17 March	8.50		

An asterisk denotes that for that period, there was a spread not exceeding ± 0.5%

Table 5 National Savings

March 1993 value of £100 of Index-linked National Savings purchased in any month since June 1975

	Jan	Feb	Mar	Apr	May	Jun	Jul	Aug	Sep	Oct	Nov	Dec
75						528.65	507.81	498.39	493.47	490.67	486.24	479.55
76	473.99	468.25	462.37	456.60	454.23	445.78	440.99	438.38	437.59	431.63	426.06	418.65
77	412.91	407.57	397.39	393.57	389.86	380.21	377.36	373.27	372.88	371.09	368.93	367.29
78	365.55	363.66	361.58	359.54	357.31	352.16	350.20	347.38	345.85	343.59	342.21	340.64
79	338.33	335.51	330.72	328.07	325.40	319.92	317.44	312.20	299.50	297.20	294.31	291.29
80	288.75	286.73	279.93	276.07	272.37	263.40	261.03	258.59	256.50	255.91	254.25	252.64
81	250.70	249.38	247.85	245.67	242.12	235.41	233.93	232.51	231.53	229.85	228.59	226.60
82	224.24	222.91	221.64	221.57	219.70	216.57	215.69	215.17	214.46	214.54	214.92	214.11
83	212.48	211.84	209.59	202.50	201.76	198.60	197.42	196.45	195.06	193.82	192.60	191.57
84	190.57	189.69	189.43	188.32	187.34	184.53	183.50	182.68	182.51	180.50	179.74	178.24
85	177.29	177.02	175.96	174.19	172.18	168.20	174.01	173.62	173.29	172.93	173.60	173.89
86	173.12	172.30	170.34	168.90	168.68	168.17	168.47	172.41	172.27	171.91	171.72	172.05
87	170.39	169.23	167.06	165.58	165.26	164.38	164.80	164.82	164.42	164.07	164.20	163.99
88	163.01	162.62	161.19	159.86	158.53	155.35	154.07	152.76	151.87	149.49	148.10	145.93
89	144.98	144.11	141.94	140.46	139.35	136.52	135.21	134.26	133.66	132.83	131.45	130.38
90	129.13	128.37	126.48	125.42	123.87	119.96	111.43	111.00	110.51	109.47	108.85	108.40
91	108.50	108.19	106.95	105.35	104.94	104.28	104.34	103.88	103.74	103.58	103.57	103.55
92	103.02	102.58	101.70									

Notes

The table gives the March 1993 value of a £100 Index-linked Certificate purchased in each of the months shown. There is no increase in value within the first year an Index-linked Certificate is held. All returns are tax-free.

The index-linked increase is based on the January 1993 Retail Price Index figure of 137.9, an increase of 1.7% over the previous year.

Retirement issue & 2nd issue

The value shown includes the index-linked increase (earned on the first of the month) and all supplements. It also includes fifth and tenth anniversary bonuses (earned on the anniversary of purchase).

Note: these Certificates are now earning index-linking only, unless the tenth anniversary bonus is still due.

3rd, 4th & 5th issues

The value shown includes the index-linked increase and any Extra Interest (both earned on the day of the month on which the certificates were purchased).

Note: after the fifth anniversary of purchase, 3rd and 4th Index-linked issues earn monthly index-linking, plus 0.5% on each following anniversary.

Non-index-linked National Savings

Following maturity, savings certificates of the 7th to 33rd issues earn interest at a variable tax-exempt General Extension Rate (3.75% as at April 1993); valuation can be obtained by writing to Savings Certificate and SAYE Office, Millburngate House, Durham DH99 1NS or by telephoning freephone 0800 868700.

Table 6 Inflation and Savings

This table illustrates the diminishing value of a £10,000 building society or bank deposit, and of the gross annual income it produces

Years since investment	A Real value of deposit	B Real value of income	C Real value of deposit	D Real value of income
0	10,000	1,100	10,000	700
1	9,434	1,038	9,804	686
2	8,900	979	9,612	673
3	8,396	924	9,423	660
4	7,921	871	9,238	647
5	7,473	822	9,057	634
6	7,050	775	8,880	622
7	6,651	732	8,706	609
8	6,274	690	8,535	597
9	5,919	651	8,368	586
10	5,584	614	8,203	574
11	5,268	579	8,043	563
12	4,970	547	7,885	552
13	4,688	516	7,730	541
14	4,423	487	7,579	531
15	4,173	459	7,430	520
16	3,936	433	7,284	510
17	3,714	409	7,142	500
18	3,503	385	7,002	490
19	3,305	364	6,864	481
20	3,118	343	6,730	471
21	2,942	324	6,598	462
22	2,775	305	6,468	453
23	2,618	288	6,342	444
24	2,470	272	6,217	435
25	2,330	256	6,095	427

The assumptions

Columns **A** & **B** give the results on the assumption of 6% inflation and 11% gross interest (not reinvested); while columns **C** & **D** give the results on the assumption of 2% inflation and 7% gross interest (again not reinvested). In neither case is account taken of tax.

Table 7   Exchange Rates

Annual average exchange rates of 20 currencies for the past 10 years

	Australia dollar	Austria schilling	Belgium franc	Canada dollar	Denmark kroner
83	1.68	27.21	77.46	1.87	13.86
84	1.52	26.64	76.96	1.73	13.80
85	1.86	26.59	76.34	1.77	13.63
86	2.20	22.37	65.47	2.04	11.86
87	2.34	20.69	61.12	2.17	11.19
88	2.28	21.97	65.38	2.19	11.97
89	2.07	21.67	64.52	1.94	11.97
90	2.29	20.24	59.44	2.08	11.01
91	2.27	20.58	60.23	2.03	11.28
92	2.40	19.36	56.64	2.13	10.63

	Europe ecu	France franc	Germany mark	Greece drachma	Holland guilder
83	1.70	11.55	3.86	132.91	4.33
84	1.69	11.64	3.79	145.56	4.27
85	1.70	11.55	3.78	179.84	4.27
86	1.49	10.16	3.18	204.74	3.59
87	1.42	9.84	2.94	221.95	3.31
88	1.51	10.60	3.12	252.34	3.52
89	1.49	10.45	3.08	265.79	3.47
90	1.40	9.69	2.88	282.36	3.24
91	1.43	9.95	2.93	321.25	3.30
92	1.36	9.32	2.75	335.46	3.10

	Hong Kong dollar	Ireland punt	Italy lira	Japan yen	Norway kroner
83	11.01	1.22	2,301.67	359.89	11.06
84	10.45	1.23	2,339.50	316.80	10.87
85	10.11	1.22	2,462.52	307.08	11.07
86	11.45	1.09	2,185.67	246.80	10.84
87	12.78	1.10	2,122.66	236.50	11.02
88	13.89	1.17	2,314.79	227.98	11.59
89	12.78	1.16	2,246.62	225.66	11.30
90	13.91	1.08	2,132.99	257.38	11.14
91	13.74	1.10	2,186.79	237.56	11.44
92	13.67	1.04	2,163.23	223.72	10.93

	Portugal escudo	Spain peseta	Sweden kroner	Switzerland franc	USA dollar
83	167.87	217.48	11.62	3.18	1.52
84	195.88	214.31	11.03	3.13	1.33
85	221.31	219.56	11.09	3.16	1.30
86	219.32	205.31	10.44	2.64	1.47
87	230.75	201.87	10.38	2.44	1.64
88	256.34	207.16	10.90	2.60	1.78
89	257.78	193.88	10.56	2.68	1.64
90	253.70	181.29	10.54	2.47	1.79
91	254.78	183.22	10.67	2.53	1.77
92	237.53	179.91	10.23	2.48	1.77

Figures denote units of currency per pound sterling

Table 8   International Living Costs

An index of comparative city living costs in April 1993

Index	City	Index	City	Index	City	Index	City
34	Bombay	87	Sydney	**100**	**London**	106	Frankfurt
58	Lagos	92	Rome	100	Madrid	113	Copenhagen
60	Rio de Janeiro	94	New York	102	Hong Kong	123	Paris
74	Abu Dhabi	97	Amsterdam	104	Brussels	184	Tokyo

Notes

Centred on London at 100, the index illustrates the cost of living in 15 cities around the world.

The ratings are based on the survey published in December 1992 by the Economist Intelligence Unit (telephone 071 493 6711), adjusted to April 1993 to reflect exchange rate movements. Surveys for these and a further 100 cities are prepared every 6 months, based on the cost of a basket of 167 goods and services including food, alcohol, tobacco, household supplies, utilities, domestic help, clothing, transport, recreation and entertainment.

Table 9   Foster Care Allowances

NFCA recommended minimum fostering allowances for the year beginning 1 April 1993

Age of child (years)	National (£ per week)	London (£ per week)
0-4	49.56	58.17
5-7	57.82	67.90
8-10	63.28	74.34
11-12	68.81	80.85
13-15	74.64	87.29
16-18	99.12	116.41

Every year the National Foster Care Association (NFCA) recommends a minimum fostering allowance for the coming year, and publishes a full survey (*Foster Care Finance*) of the allowances paid by each local authority. The NFCA recommended allowance varies according to the age of the child and whether or not the placement is in London. *Foster Care Finance* may be purchased from the NFCA, Leonard House, 5-7 Marshalsea Road, London SE1 1EP (telephone 071 828 6266).

Table 10   Car Running Costs

Total car running and maintenance costs according to engine capacity

Cost per mile (pence)

Annual mileage	Engine capacity (cc)				
	up to 1,000	1,001 to 1,400	1,401 to 2,000	2,001 to 3,000	3,001 to 4,500
5,000	45.93	59.21	74.68	123.26	149.26
10,000	29.48	36.77	45.59	73.53	89.06
15,000	25.11	30.95	38.23	61.34	74.70
20,000	23.76	29.30	36.30	58.53	71.81
25,000	22.94	28.31	35.14	56.85	70.08
30,000	21.29	25.98	32.04	51.34	63.21

The assumptions

Insurance is average cost of fully comprehensive policy, undiscounted

Depreciation is based on average cost of a new car for 8 years/80,000 miles

AA membership includes Relay service

Petrol is unleaded petrol at 50.00p per litre/£2.27 per gallon:
note that the AA no longer produces figures for leaded petrol

Tyres have estimated life of 30,000 miles

Servicing is routine servicing costs; older cars may have greater costs

Repairs and renovations estimated on total costs over 8 years/80,000 miles

Table 10   Car Running Costs

Figures in the tables *left* have been calculated from the information in the tables below

Standing charges: cost per annum (£)

	Engine capacity (cc)				
	up to 1,000	1,001 to 1,400	1,401 to 2,000	2,001 to 3,000	3,001 to 4,500
Car licence	125.00	125.00	125.00	125.00	125.00
Insurance	622.49	802.45	968.00	1,495.10	1,544.53
Depreciation	833.50	1,253.13	1,752.02	3,288.88	4,287.00
AA subscription	64.00	64.00	64.00	64.00	64.00
Totals	1,644.99	2,244.58	2,909.02	4,972.98	6,020.53

Standing charges: cost per mile (pence)

Annual mileage	Engine capacity (cc)				
	up to 1,000	1,001 to 1,400	1,401 to 2,000	2,001 to 3,000	3,001 to 4,500
5,000	32.90	44.89	58.18	99.46	120.41
10,000	16.45	22.45	29.09	49.73	60.21
15,000	12.08	16.63	21.73	37.54	45.85
20,000	10.73	14.98	19.80	34.73	42.96
25,000	9.91	13.99	18.64	33.05	41.23
30,000	8.26	11.66	15.54	27.54	34.36

Running costs: cost per mile (pence)

	Engine capacity (cc)				
	up to 1,000	1,001 to 1,400	1,401 to 2,000	2,001 to 3,000	3,001 to 4,500
Petrol	5.69	6.50	7.58	10.34	11.37
Oil	0.53	0.53	0.57	0.63	1.03
Tyres	0.61	0.80	0.97	1.86	2.40
Servicing	1.20	1.20	1.20	1.62	2.43
Repairs & replacements	5.00	5.29	6.18	9.35	11.62
Totals	13.03	14.32	16.50	23.80	28.85
For each 1p change in the cost per litre of petrol, add/subtract	0.11	0.13	0.15	0.21	0.23

Table 11   School Fees

Range of termly fees each year for various types of independent school

| Year | Pre-prep (3-8) | Junior school (8-13) | | Senior school (11-18) | | | |
| | Boys and girls | Boys and girls | | Girls' schools | | Boys' schools | |
	Day	Day	Boarding	Day	Boarding	Day	Boarding
83	100-200	300-950	700-1,225	425-900	775-1,450	300-1,200	800-1,600
84	100-200	330-980	700-1,480	430-1,030	830-1,530	300-1,300	830-1,900
85	100-200	350-1,055	730-1,600	490-1,120	870-1,610	325-1,400	880-2,025
86	100-300	350-1,100	800-1,650	500-1,150	1,000-1,700	360-1,500	950-2,200
87	150-350	350-1,500	800-1,950	500-1,300	1,000-2,000	500-2,000	1,000-2,250
88	150-400	350-1,500	800-1,800	500-1,350	1,100-2,100	500-1,750	1,100-2,350
89	200-500	350-1,500	900-2,000	600-1,500	1,350-2,400	600-2,000	1,200-2,800
90	250-550	450-1,550	1,100-2,150	800-1,600	1,600-2,600	800-2,100	1,400-2,900
91	300-700	600-1,650	1,300-2,500	900-1,900	1,900-3,400	900-2,500	1,900-3,600
92	300-700	600-1,900	1,400-2,800	1,000-2,100	2,100-3,500	1,000-2,600	2,100-3,700

Rate of increase

Analysis of the rate of increase in school fees between 1983 and 1992 (Table A *below*) shows an average increase for all schools (excluding pre-prep) of **14.5% p.a.** Average annual inflation over the period was 6.4% p.a., so as a rule of thumb it is reasonable to project a **real rate of increase** in school fees of **8.0% p.a.** They will therefore cost the person paying the fees 8% more each year in real terms. ISIS (the Independent Schools Information Service) predict an 8% increase in 1993.

An example showing the effect of this real rate of increase on a man with an initial net income of £40,000 is given in Table B *below*.

Table B assumptions

Net income increases by 4% annually

School fees increase by 12% annually

Table A

Category	Average annual increase
Pre-prep	25.9%
Junior day school	11.1%
Junior boarding school	13.1%
Senior schools	
Girls' day schools	14.9%
Girls' boarding schools	16.9%
Boys' day schools	15.6%
Boys' boarding schools	15.7%

Table B

Year	Net income (£)	School fees (£)	% of income paid
1	40,000	5,000	12.5
2	41,600	5,600	13.5
3	43,264	6,272	14.5
4	44,995	7,025	15.6
5	46,794	7,868	16.8
6	48,666	8,812	18.1
7	50,613	9,869	19.5
8	52,637	11,053	21.0

Table 12   House Price Indices

Standardised indices showing change in property prices since 1985

UK indices (by property type)

Year	All houses			New houses			Existing houses		
	Index	*%*	*Av'ge price*	*Index*	*%*	*Av'ge price*	*Index*	*%*	*Av'ge price*
85	117.0	9.1	32,953	115.4	8.0	37,357	117.3	9.5	32,393
86	129.9	11.0	38,693	126.6	9.6	44,749	130.6	11.4	38,010
87	149.9	15.4	47,482	141.9	12.1	54,411	151.6	16.0	46,661
88	184.8	23.3	57,594	175.4	23.6	67,535	186.7	23.2	56,424
89	223.1	20.8	61,163	206.2	17.6	73,561	226.5	21.3	59,278
90	223.2	0.0	64,729	207.8	0.8	77,405	225.8	(0.3)	62,903
91	220.5	(1.2)	68,130	204.0	(1.8)	70,987	223.1	(1.2)	67,717
92	208.1	(5.6)	64,309	197.2	(5.8)	68,634	210.2	(5.8)	63,797

Regional indices (all houses)

Year	North		Yorks/Humb.		N. West		E. Midlands		W. Midlands		E. Anglia	
	Index	*%*	*Index*	*%*	*Index*	*%*	*Index*	*%*	*Index*	*%*	*Index*	*%*
85	109.6	4.6	112.0	5.6	110.1	6.0	116.6	9.1	109.7	5.6	121.2	11.8
86	114.5	4.5	119.6	6.8	118.9	8.0	126.8	8.7	119.4	8.9	138.9	14.6
87	122.0	6.5	130.5	9.1	127.9	7.6	145.2	14.6	136.9	14.6	174.1	25.3
88	136.7	12.1	155.0	18.8	149.0	16.5	187.3	28.8	185.8	35.7	248.9	43.0
89	182.8	33.7	222.7	43.6	202.0	35.5	243.2	30.0	240.7	29.6	255.5	2.6
90	207.7	13.6	237.5	6.6	227.4	12.6	234.4	(3.6)	238.0	(1.1)	225.8	(11.6)
91	213.5	2.8	240.4	1.2	236.3	3.9	227.9	(2.8)	240.4	1.0	214.4	(5.0)
92	210.1	(1.6)	231.9	(3.6)	226.1	(4.3)	214.4	(5.9)	229.4	(4.6)	198.5	(7.4)

Year	S. West		S. East.		Gr. London		Wales		Scotland		N. Ireland	
	Index	*%*	*Index*	*%*	*Index*	*%*	*Index*	*%*	*Index*	*%*	*Index*	*%*
85	117.7	10.7	123.9	13.0	131.2	17.6	111.1	6.3	115.9	6.3	114.1	5.7
86	131.6	11.8	144.3	16.5	159.6	21.6	118.3	6.6	119.9	3.4	121.4	6.4
87	158.1	20.2	181.0	25.4	200.6	25.7	130.4	10.2	126.8	5.8	121.5	0.1
88	217.6	37.6	232.4	28.4	245.3	22.3	162.3	24.5	139.7	10.2	126.7	4.2
89	242.7	11.5	244.3	5.1	251.1	2.3	215.5	32.8	165.0	18.1	130.6	3.1
90	221.8	(8.6)	224.5	(8.1)	236.6	(5.8)	219.6	1.9	182.1	10.4	132.1	1.1
91	210.4	(5.0)	210.8	(6.1)	222.9	(5.8)	217.1	(1.1)	192.8	5.9	146.9	11.2
92	193.9	(7.8)	192.8	(8.5)	202.0	(9.4)	207.7	(4.3)	193.2	0.2	145.5	(1.0)

Index 1983 = 100
% = Percentage change in index from preceding year
Figures in brackets indicate a fall in the index
Region = Economic planning region

The Index is calculated by reference to transactions involving a limited number of carefully chosen individual properties, whereas the average price is a crude figure calculated from the building society's new mortgage business in each period and region. There is thus no correlation between the movements in the Index and the changes in average prices, and the Index is the measure to be relied upon in making comparisons.

Table 13 Valuing Shares

This table may be used in order to achieve a very rough estimate of the value of a shareholding in a family company.

The formula used is
  a   Maintainable future post-tax profits
× **b**   P/E ratio on FT-Actuaries Index for relevant industry sector or on FT-Actuaries 500 Index (consult current *Financial Times* or a stockbroker)
× **c**   Percentage interest in the company
× **d**   Adjustment for size of company, size of shareholding, marketability and lack of dividend in accordance with the table *below*

It is very important to note that if the husband were to sell his shares for the amount given by this formula, then capital gains tax would be payable on any gain in real value since acquisition (or since March 1982 if later). Such latent tax must be calculated and subtracted from the gross figure given by the formula. Table 21 will prove helpful in establishing the amount of capital gains tax, although where the shares were held at March 1982 it may be necessary to undertake a further valuation as at that time.

For the full text of the article upon which this table is based see *Between Scylla and Charybdis: How to value, very broadly, shares in the family company* [1993] Fam Law 113.

	Post-tax profit (£'000)				
Size of shareholding	**under 100**	**100–200**	**200–500**	**500–1,000**	**over 1,000**
under 10%	25%	30%	35%	40%	40%
10% – 25%	30%	40%	45%	50%	50%
25.1% – 49.9%	35%	45%	50%	60%	65%
50%	40%	50%	60%	70%	75%
50.1% – 74.9%	45%	55%	65%	75%	85%
75% and over	55%	65%	80%	90%	100%

Worked example

The husband owns 60% of a computer/electronics company. There is no reason to expect a significant variation in the future pattern of profitability, and the profits represent a reasonable return on capital employed in the business.

The recent profit record, before exceptional items and after a normal tax charge, is

1990	£106,000
1991	£72,000
1992	£85,000

The simple average over these years is £87,667. This figure, being higher than the most recent year's profit, is therefore taken to establish maintainable future profits.

On consulting the *Financial Times* it is found that the electronics sector of the FT-Actuaries Index shows a ratio of 14.50, and the FT-Actuaries 500 Index shows an historic P/E ratio of 14.64.

A rough estimate of the husband's interest in the company is therefore

      a   £87,667
    × **b**   say 14.50 = £1,271,151
    × **c**   60% = £762,702
    × **d**   45% = £343,216

or say **£350,000** to the nearest £25,000.

Table 14 Endowment Premiums

With-profits endowment: monthly premium for a male, sum assured plus any attaching bonuses payable on survival to the end of the term or on earlier death

Age	Term in years								
	10	15	20	25	30	35	40	45	50
20	474.00	307.50	236.00	194.00	169.00	154.50	145.50	134.00	125.00
25	474.00	307.50	236.00	194.50	170.00	155.50	147.50	136.50	128.50
30	474.50	308.50	237.50	196.50	172.50	158.50	151.50	141.50	134.50
35	475.50	310.00	239.50	199.50	176.00	163.00	157.00	148.50	143.50
40	477.00	312.50	243.00	204.00	182.00	170.50	166.00	159.50	156.00
45	480.00	316.50	248.00	211.50	191.00	182.00	179.50	175.50	173.50
50	485.00	324.00	258.00	223.50	206.50	200.00	200.00	198.00	197.00
55	403.50	336.00	274.00	244.50	231.00	227.50	230.00	229.00	229.00
60	507.50	356.00	300.50	277.00	268.00	288.00	272.00	271.50	
65	530.00	388.00	342.00	327.50	323.50	325.50	330.00		

These monthly premiums are for a sum assured of £50,000 based on figures quoted by Royal Life in March 1993.

Monthly premium charged is in proportion with the sum assured.
For example, the monthly premium for a sum assured of £75,000 for a male aged 25 over a 30 year term would be £170.00 (see table) × (£75,000÷£50,000) = £170.00 × 1.5 = £255.00

A policy charge of £1.50 is added to each policy (additional to the above premiums).

The above age is applied to males. Females can use the above table noting that female age is equivalent to the male age less four years.

Low-cost endowment: monthly premium for a male, sum assured plus any attaching bonuses on survival to the end of the term, or a guaranteed death benefit on earlier death

Age	Term in years						
	10	15	20	25	30	35	40
20	348.00	181.50	107.00	65.50	41.50	38.00	35.00
25	348.00	181.50	107.00	66.00	42.00	39.00	37.00
30	348.00	182.00	108.50	67.00	44.50	41.00	39.50
35	349.00	183.50	110.00	70.00	47.50	44.00	43.00
40	351.00	185.50	113.00	74.00	52.50	49.50	48.50
45	353.50	189.50	118.50	80.50	60.50	58.00	57.50
50	358.50	196.50	127.50	92.00	74.00	72.50	72.50
55	367.00	208.50	142.50	111.00	96.00	95.00	95.50
60	381.00	228.00	167.50	141.50	130.00	130.00	131.00
65	403.50	259.00	207.50	189.00	181.50	182.00	183.50

The above monthly premiums are for a guaranteed death benefit of £50,000, based on figures quoted by Royal Life in March 1993.

Monthly premium charged is in proportion with the guaranteed death benefit.
For example, the monthly premium for a guaranteed death benefit of £30,000 for a male aged 35 over a 25 year term would be £70 (see table) × (£30,000÷£50,000) = £70 × 0.6 = £42

A policy charge of £1.50 is added to each policy (additional to the above premiums).

The above age is applied to males. Females can use the above table noting that female age is equivalent to the male age less four years.

Table 15   Mortgage Repayments

This table shows the initial annual cost of a repayment mortgage after basic rate tax relief

25 year term

Initial borrowing	Mortgage interest rate										
	5%	*6%*	*7%*	*8%*	*9%*	*10%*	*11%*	*12%*	*13%*	*14%*	*15%*
10,000	585	632	683	737	793	852	912	975	1,039	1,105	1,172
20,000	1,169	1,265	1,366	1,474	1,586	1,703	1,825	1,950	2,079	2,210	2,344
30,000	1,754	1,897	2,049	2,210	2,379	2,555	2,737	2,925	3,118	3,315	3,516
40,000	2,463	2,679	2,907	3,147	3,397	3,657	3,925	4,200	4,482	4,770	5,063
50,000	3,173	3,461	3,766	4,084	4,415	4,758	5,112	5,475	5,846	6,225	6,610
60,000	3,882	4,244	4,624	5,021	5,433	5,860	6,299	6,750	7,211	7,680	8,157
70,000	4,592	5,026	5,482	5,958	6,451	6,962	7,487	8,025	8,575	9,135	9,704
80,000	5,301	5,808	6,340	6,894	7,470	8,063	8,674	9,300	9,939	10,590	11,251
100,000	6,720	7,373	8,056	8,768	9,506	10,267	11,049	11,850	12,668	13,500	14,345
150,000	10,268	11,284	12,347	13,452	14,596	15,775	16,986	18,225	19,489	20,775	22,080
200,000	13,815	15,195	16,637	18,136	19,686	21,284	22,923	24,600	26,310	28,050	29,815

20 year term

Initial borrowing	Mortgage interest rate										
	5%	*6%*	*7%*	*8%*	*9%*	*10%*	*11%*	*12%*	*13%*	*14%*	*15%*
10,000	677	722	769	819	870	925	981	1,039	1,099	1,160	1,223
20,000	1,355	1,444	1,538	1,637	1,741	1,849	1,962	2,078	2,197	2,320	2,445
30,000	2,032	2,166	2,307	2,456	2,611	2,774	2,942	3,116	3,296	3,480	3,668
40,000	2,835	3,037	3,251	3,474	3,707	3,948	4,198	4,455	4,719	4,989	5,265
50,000	3,637	3,909	4,195	4,493	4,802	5,123	5,454	5,794	6,143	6,499	6,863
60,000	4,440	4,781	5,139	5,511	5,898	6,298	6,710	7,133	7,566	8,009	8,461
70,000	5,242	5,653	6,083	6,530	6,993	7,472	7,965	8,472	8,990	9,519	10,058
80,000	6,044	6,525	7,026	7,548	8,089	8,647	9,221	9,810	10,413	11,029	11,656
100,000	7,649	8,268	8,914	9,585	10,280	10,996	11,733	12,488	13,260	14,049	14,851
150,000	11,661	12,628	13,634	14,678	15,757	16,869	18,011	19,182	20,378	21,598	22,839
200,000	15,674	16,987	18,354	19,770	21,234	22,742	24,290	25,876	27,496	29,147	30,827

15 year term

Initial borrowing	Mortgage interest rate										
	5%	*6%*	*7%*	*8%*	*9%*	*10%*	*11%*	*12%*	*13%*	*14%*	*15%*
10,000	838	880	923	968	1,016	1,065	1,116	1,168	1,222	1,278	1,335
20,000	1,677	1,759	1,846	1,937	2,031	2,129	2,231	2,336	2,445	2,556	2,670
30,000	2,515	2,639	2,769	2,905	3,047	3,194	3,347	3,505	3,667	3,834	4,006
40,000	3,479	3,669	3,867	4,073	4,287	4,509	4,738	4,973	5,215	5,462	5,716
50,000	4,442	4,698	4,965	5,241	5,528	5,824	6,128	6,441	6,762	7,090	7,426
60,000	5,406	5,728	6,063	6,410	6,769	7,138	7,519	7,909	8,310	8,719	9,136
70,000	6,369	6,757	7,161	7,578	8,009	8,453	8,910	9,378	9,857	10,347	10,846
80,000	7,332	7,787	8,259	8,746	9,250	9,768	10,300	10,846	11,404	11,975	12,556
100,000	9,259	9,846	10,454	11,083	11,731	12,397	13,082	13,782	14,499	15,231	15,977
150,000	14,076	14,994	15,944	16,924	17,934	18,971	20,035	21,124	22,236	23,371	24,528
200,000	18,893	20,143	21,434	22,766	24,137	25,545	26,988	28,465	29,973	31,512	33,078

Basic rate tax relief on up to the current maximum of £30,000 has been allowed for.

The net annual cost will increase progressively over the mortgage term as the capital outstanding decreases.

Thus the interest payable and the tax relief referable thereto both reduce each year. Some illustrations of the increasing percentage of principal repayment (over a 25 year term) are shown *opposite*.

Table 15 Mortgage Repayments

The percentage (%) of net payment which is principal over a 25 year term

Year	£10,000	£20,000	£30,000	£40,000	£50,000	£60,000
1	18.57	18.57	18.57	17.39	16.75	16.35
2	19.98	19.98	19.98	18.78	18.09	17.65
3	21.49	21.49	21.49	20.28	19.53	19.07
4	23.11	23.11	23.11	21.90	21.10	20.59
5	24.84	24.84	24.84	23.65	22.78	22.24
6	26.70	26.70	26.70	25.55	24.61	24.02
7	28.68	28.68	28.68	27.59	26.58	25.94
8	30.80	30.80	30.80	29.80	28.70	28.02
9	33.06	33.06	33.06	32.18	31.00	30.26
10	35.47	35.47	35.47	34.75	33.48	32.68
11	38.04	38.04	38.04	37.53	36.16	35.29
12	40.77	40.77	40.77	40.54	39.05	38.11
13	43.67	43.67	43.67	43.67	42.17	41.16
14	46.76	46.76	46.76	46.76	45.55	44.46
15	50.03	50.03	50.03	50.03	49.19	48.01
16	53.50	53.50	53.50	53.50	53.12	51.85
17	57.17	57.17	57.17	57.17	57.17	56.00
18	61.04	61.04	61.04	61.04	61.04	60.48
19	65.13	65.13	65.13	65.13	65.13	65.13
20	69.44	69.44	69.44	69.44	69.44	69.44
21	73.96	73.96	73.96	73.96	73.96	73.96
22	78.72	78.72	78.72	78.72	78.72	78.72
23	83.70	83.70	83.70	83.70	83.70	83.70
24	88.90	88.90	88.90	88.90	88.90	88.90
25	94.34	94.34	94.34	94.34	94.34	94.34

Year	£70,000	£80,000	£90,000	£100,000	£150,000	£200,000
1	16.07	15.87	15.72	15.60	15.25	15.08
2	17.36	17.14	16.98	16.85	16.47	16.29
3	18.75	18.51	18.34	18.20	17.79	17.59
4	20.25	19.99	19.80	19.65	19.21	19.00
5	21.87	21.59	21.39	21.23	20.75	20.52
6	23.62	23.32	23.10	22.92	22.41	22.16
7	25.50	25.19	24.95	24.76	24.20	23.94
8	27.55	27.20	26.94	26.74	26.14	25.85
9	29.75	29.38	29.10	28.88	28.23	27.92
10	32.13	31.73	31.43	31.19	30.49	30.15
11	34.70	34.27	33.94	33.68	32.93	32.57
12	37.47	37.01	36.65	36.38	35.56	35.17
13	40.47	39.97	39.59	39.29	38.41	37.99
14	43.71	43.17	42.75	42.43	41.48	41.03
15	47.21	46.62	46.17	45.82	44.80	44.31
16	50.98	50.35	49.87	49.49	48.39	47.85
17	55.06	54.38	53.86	53.45	52.26	51.68
18	59.47	58.73	58.17	57.72	56.44	55.81
19	64.23	63.43	62.82	62.34	60.95	60.28
20	69.36	68.50	67.85	67.33	65.83	65.10
21	73.96	73.96	73.72	72.72	71.09	70.31
22	78.72	78.72	78.72	78.53	76.78	75.93
23	83.70	83.70	83.70	83.70	82.92	82.01
24	88.90	88.90	88.90	88.90	88.90	88.57
25	94.34	94.34	94.34	94.34	94.34	94.34

All calculations are based on net payments, at a mortgage rate of 8.00% with MIRAS available on the first £30,000, and assume a basic rate of tax of 25%.

For any two mortgages with the same rate of interest under £30,000 (debt outstanding) the element of principal in any given year will be the same.

For further information contact the Group Planning and Research Department of the Halifax Building Society by telephoning 0422 333333.

Table 16   Annuity Rates

Gross annuity for each £1,000 of purchase money payable monthly in advance to a female for her life

Age	Escalating at 0% p.a.		Escalating at 3% p.a.		Escalating at 5% p.a.	
	Gross payment	Capital content	Gross payment	Capital content	Gross payment	Capital content
30	64.08	19.08	38.52	3.04	23.52	4.08
35	65.16	21.00	40.08	9.00	25.32	5.04
40	66.72	23.04	42.12	11.04	27.60	6.00
45	68.88	26.04	44.76	13.08	30.60	8.04
50	71.88	30.00	48.24	16.08	34.20	10.08
55	75.96	34.08	52.92	20.04	39.12	14.04
60	81.96	40.08	59.28	26.04	45.60	19.08
65	90.36	49.08	68.04	33.00	54.48	25.08

Notes

1 The rates quoted are not guaranteed. They are subject to market fluctuations and are sensitive to interest rates. The table shows rates supplied by The Equitable Life on 15 April 1993. Quotations for more sophisticated annuities (e.g. index-linked, with profits, guaranteed for a minimum term of years) are available in the market.

2 The tables make no allowance for income tax on the taxable element (the gross payment less the capital content), which for each annuitant will depend on relevant personal circumstances: see Table 20.

3 Intervening ages can be approximately interpolated. For male annuitants the tables can be applied by adopting the figures for a female about 4 years older than the male in question.

Table 17   Life Expectancy

Further life expectancy in years according to age and sex

	Male							Female							
	20	30	40	50	60	70	80	20	30	40	50	60	70	80	
0	52	43	33	24	16	10	6	58	48	39	29	21	13	7	0
1	52	42	32	23	16	10	5	57	47	38	29	20	13	7	1
2	51	41	31	23	15	9	5	56	46	37	28	19	12	7	2
3	50	40	31	22	14	9	5	55	45	36	27	19	11	6	3
4	49	39	30	21	14	8	5	54	44	35	26	18	11	6	4
5	48	38	29	20	13	8	4	53	43	34	25	17	10	5	5
6	47	37	28	19	12	7	4	52	43	33	24	16	10	5	6
7	46	36	27	19	12	7	4	51	42	32	23	16	9	5	7
8	45	35	26	18	11	6	4	50	41	31	23	15	9	4	8
9	44	34	25	17	11	6	4	49	40	30	22	14	8	4	9

To find life expectancy choose column according to sex, and age in tens of years:
then look down to find appropriate row according to units of years

Example: for a 33-year-old **Female**, look to the intersection of **30** column and **3** row to find figure of 45:
this gives the actuarial expectation of death at the age of 78 (33 + 45)

Caveat: this table follows *English Life Tables No.14* (ELT14) prepared by the Government Actuary, based on statistics for the general population of England and Wales from 1980-82. Note that the life expectancy of professional people is actuarially higher than for the general population. The table which appeared in the first edition of *At a Glance*, derived from table PA90 prepared by the Faculty & Institute of Actuaries, was based on statistics for pensioners in insured pension schemes, whose life expectancy is also greater than that of the population taken as a whole.

For the reasons discussed in the preface that more optimistic table PA90 remains the basis for the life expectancy column used in the **Duxbury** calculations which follow *overleaf*, and is thus an element in their computation.

Table 18   Duxbury Calculations

Capitalising maintenance: capital required (to nearest £1,000) to fund a wife's net income need for life

Age of wife	Life expectancy	£10,000	£12,000	£14,000	£16,000	£18,000	£20,000	£25,000
42	39	164,000	203,000	241,000	279,000	318,000	357,000	453,000
43	38	161,000	199,000	237,000	275,000	313,000	352,000	447,000
44	37	159,000	196,000	233,000	272,000	309,000	347,000	441,000
45	36	155,000	193,000	230,000	267,000	304,000	342,000	435,000
46	35	152,000	189,000	225,000	263,000	299,000	337,000	428,000
47	34	150,000	186,000	222,000	258,000	294,000	331,000	421,000
48	33	146,000	182,000	217,000	253,000	289,000	324,000	414,000
49	32	143,000	178,000	213,000	248,000	283,000	319,000	406,000
50	31	139,000	173,000	209,000	242,000	277,000	312,000	399,000
51	31	138,000	172,000	207,000	241,000	276,000	310,000	397,000
52	30	134,000	168,000	202,000	235,000	269,000	304,000	389,000
53	29	130,000	164,000	196,000	230,000	264,000	297,000	380,000
54	28	126,000	159,000	191,000	225,000	257,000	289,000	371,000
55	27	122,000	154,000	186,000	218,000	250,000	282,000	362,000
56	26	118,000	149,000	180,000	211,000	243,000	275,000	352,000
57	25	113,000	144,000	174,000	205,000	236,000	266,000	343,000
58	24	109,000	139,000	168,000	199,000	228,000	258,000	332,000
59	23	104,000	133,000	162,000	191,000	220,000	249,000	322,000
60	23	102,000	131,000	160,000	189,000	218,000	248,000	320,000
62	21	96,000	123,000	151,000	179,000	206,000	233,000	301,000
64	19	90,000	115,000	141,000	167,000	192,000	218,000	282,000
66	18	86,000	111,000	136,000	160,000	186,000	210,000	272,000
68	16	79,000	102,000	125,000	148,000	170,000	194,000	250,000
70	15	76,000	98,000	119,000	141,000	163,000	185,000	238,000
72	13	68,000	88,000	107,000	126,000	146,000	166,000	214,000
74	12	64,000	82,000	100,000	119,000	137,000	156,000	201,000
76	11	60,000	77,000	94,000	111,000	128,000	145,000	187,000

In **B v B** [1990] 1 FLR 20 Ward J stated, at page 24E-G: 'The Duxbury calculation was conceived to address the observations of the Court of Appeal in **Preston v Preston** [1982] Fam 17. There the Court of Appeal pointed out firstly that the recipient of the lump sum is expected to expend it, or so much of it as is intended to meet future income needs, by drawing both upon its capital as well as relying upon the income it can produce. Secondly, that help should be provided to the court by accountants or investment consultants, or even by reference to annuity tables, to show the court how the lump sum could be thus applied. As a result of Preston the practice has grown up for accountants to devise a computer program which can calculate the lump sum which, if invested on the assumptions as to life expectancy, rates of inflation, return on investment, growth of capital, incidence of income tax, will produce enough to meet the recipient's needs for her life . . . I have concluded that, if this calculation is accepted as no more than a tool for the judge's use, then it is a very valuable help to him in many cases'.

In **Gojkovic v Gojkovic** [1992] Fam 40, Butler-Sloss LJ stated, at page 48E:
'. . . a Duxbury calculation cannot by itself provide the answer as to the sum to which the wife is entitled, though it produces a figure to which the judge is entitled to have regard in deciding what is the right answer'.

Note: the figures in this table are lower than those given in the first edition of *At a Glance* to reflect the lower rate of income yield assumed, and the increase in state pension. Life expectancy is based on the same table PA90 (prepared by the Faculty & Institute of Actuaries) as in the first edition, for the reasons discussed in the preface.

Table 18 Duxbury Calculations

£30,000	£35,000	£40,000	£50,000	£60,000	£80,000	£100,000	Life expectancy	Age of wife
550,000	650,000	754,000	967,000	1,180,000	1,609,000	2,040,000	39	42
543,000	641,000	744,000	953,000	1,164,000	1,587,000	2,011,000	38	43
536,000	632,000	733,000	939,000	1,147,000	1,565,000	1,983,000	37	44
528,000	623,000	722,000	925,000	1,129,000	1,541,000	1,953,000	36	45
520,000	614,000	710,000	910,000	1,112,000	1,516,000	1,921,000	35	46
512,000	604,000	699,000	895,000	1,093,000	1,492,000	1,890,000	34	47
503,000	593,000	687,000	879,000	1,074,000	1,465,000	1,857,000	33	48
494,000	582,000	674,000	864,000	1,055,000	1,439,000	1,824,000	32	49
484,000	571,000	661,000	847,000	1,034,000	1,411,000	1,789,000	31	50
484,000	570,000	659,000	845,000	1,033,000	1,410,000	1,788,000	31	51
474,000	559,000	647,000	828,000	1,012,000	1,381,000	1,752,000	30	52
464,000	546,000	633,000	810,000	990,000	1,352,000	1,714,000	29	53
453,000	535,000	618,000	792,000	968,000	1,321,000	1,676,000	28	54
443,000	522,000	603,000	773,000	944,000	1,290,000	1,637,000	27	55
431,000	509,000	589,000	754,000	920,000	1,258,000	1,596,000	26	56
419,000	496,000	574,000	734,000	896,000	1,225,000	1,554,000	25	57
407,000	482,000	557,000	713,000	871,000	1,190,000	1,511,000	24	58
395,000	467,000	540,000	692,000	845,000	1,156,000	1,467,000	23	59
392,000	465,000	539,000	690,000	843,000	1,154,000	1,465,000	23	60
370,000	439,000	508,000	649,000	793,000	1,084,000	1,375,000	21	62
346,000	410,000	475,000	605,000	738,000	1,008,000	1,280,000	19	64
333,000	395,000	457,000	583,000	710,000	969,000	1,230,000	18	66
306,000	364,000	421,000	534,000	651,000	887,000	1,125,000	16	68
292,000	347,000	401,000	510,000	620,000	844,000	1,070,000	15	70
262,000	311,000	360,000	457,000	554,000	754,000	956,000	13	72
246,000	293,000	338,000	429,000	520,000	707,000	895,000	12	74
230,000	273,000	315,000	400,000	486,000	658,000	833,000	11	76

The assumptions

The columns in the table relate to an initial annual net income requirement for the wife, calculated after tax at 1993-94 rates. The table assumes that the wife has no other income (save the state pension from age 60).

The figures in the table assume an income yield of 5 per cent, capital growth of 4 per cent, and inflation of 4 per cent.

Thus the assumed real rate of return is 5 per cent (being the difference between the rate of inflation and the aggregated rates of income yield and capital growth). It is true that in **B v B** (*ibid*) Ward J suggested that a real rate of return of 4 per cent should be used, but the commonly adopted practice is to take the figure of 5 per cent.

The computer program permits other variables to be introduced, such as earned income and external capital receipts. For example, the calculation for a 51-year-old woman to receive £20,000 per annum is £310,000. If she can earn, say, £7,500 per annum gross until her retirement, then the figure would fall to £268,000. It is not possible to create a table encompassing all such permutations and it is suggested that where external income or capital may arise an individual calculation should be obtained.

Table 19   Value of Lost Pension

A divorce will usually cause a woman to lose the chance of acquiring widow's benefits from her husband's pension. Under s.25 (2) (h) of the Matrimonial Causes Act 1973, these lost benefits are to be taken into account, but often the court either disregards them as 'too remote' or invokes them to justify an otherwise unsustainable award.

Actuarial techniques can be used to estimate the value of these potentially lost pension rights. The approach is to work out the widow's pension based on the husband's current pensionable salary and his expected length of service, and then to adjust the resulting figure to give the prima facie lump sum to be paid to the wife by way of compensation for the loss of that benefit. The adjustment is in the form of two multipliers.

The first multiplier (Table A *opposite*) is the cost at the husband's normal retirement date of buying £1 of widow's pension payable to her on the death of her husband after retirement. There are two factors that affect the first multiplier: the age difference between husband and wife, and the possibility that the pension scheme allows for increase in pensions once in payment. The multipliers in table A cater for three pension scheme situations: 0% p.a. (i.e. no increases in payment), 3% p.a. and 5% p.a.

The second multiplier (Table B *opposite)* compensates for the payment of the lump sum **now** rather than on the husband's normal retirement date. This discount multiplier takes into account not only expected income and capital growth from such a lump sum, but also expected increases in the husband's earnings, and makes allowance for the possibility of both husband and wife dying before retirement.

In summary:

Prima facie lump sum = Widow's pension ×
                            Table A multiplier ×
                            Table B multiplier

For full text and formulae used in compiling these tables, see *What price a widow's mite?* (1991) Fam Law 8

The assumptions

Husband's retirement date is his 65th birthday: if he retires on his 60th birthday, a rough adjustment would be to work the calculations on the basis of retiring at age 65 and then **increase** the resulting figure by 20%

No account has been taken of taxation

Effect of the pension scheme being used to contract husband out of the state scheme is ignored

Benefits that may be payable on husband's death in service are ignored

Husband will receive salary increases not markedly out of line with the rate for non-manual workers

Husband and wife both in good health (if husband in poor health, value of lost benefit will be **greater**; if wife in poor health, **smaller**)

Table 19   Value of Lost Pension

Table A

Husband's age minus wife's age	Multiplier 1 Pension increases in payment at		
	0% p.a.	3% p.a.	5% p.a.
10	2.71	4.45	6.37
9	2.64	4.30	6.12
8	2.57	4.15	5.86
7	2.49	3.99	5.60
6	2.42	3.84	5.35
5	2.34	3.68	5.09
4	2.26	3.52	4.84
3	2.17	3.36	4.59
2	2.09	3.20	4.34
1	2.01	3.05	4.10
0	1.92	2.89	3.86
−1	1.84	2.73	3.62
−2	1.75	2.58	3.39
−3	1.66	2.43	3.17
−4	1.58	2.28	2.96
−5	1.49	2.14	2.75

Table B

Age of husband	Multiplier 2	Age of husband	Multiplier 2
25	0.23	45	0.43
26	0.24	46	0.45
27	0.25	47	0.46
28	0.26	48	0.48
29	0.26	49	0.49
30	0.27	50	0.51
31	0.28	51	0.53
32	0.29	52	0.55
33	0.30	53	0.57
34	0.31	54	0.59
35	0.32	55	0.62
36	0.33	56	0.64
37	0.34	57	0.67
38	0.35	58	0.70
39	0.36	59	0.73
40	0.37	60	0.77
41	0.38	61	0.81
42	0.39	62	0.85
43	0.41	63	0.89
44	0.42	64	0.94

Worked example

H is 52 and W is 48. H has 15 years pensionable service to date and will have 28 on normal retirement date (when 65). H's current salary is £24,000. Scheme provides for 1/60th of final salary for each service year and a widow's pension on his death after retirement of 50% of the member's pension. All pensions increase by 3% p.a. in payment.

His expected pension at retirement, based on current salary, is
28/60 × £24,000 = **£11,200 p.a.**

The widow's pension, on this basis, is
50% × £11,200 = **£5,600 p.a.**

Table A multiplier for age difference (H-W) = (52−48) = 4 years and a pension with 3% increase is **3.52**

Table B multiplier for a man aged 52 is **0.55**

Hence an estimate for the prima facie lump sum to be paid by way of compensation is

Widow's pension × Table A multiplier × Table B multiplier

£5,600 × 3.52 × 0.55 = **£10,842**

Table 20   Income Tax

	Fiscal year						
	87-88	*88-89*	*89-90*	*90-91*	*91-92*	*92-93*	*93-94*
Income Tax Reliefs							
Personal allowance	—	—	—	3,005	3,295	3,445	3,445
Married couple's allowance	—	—	—	1,720	1,720	1,720	1,720
Previous personal allowances							
Single	2,425	2,605	2,785	—	—	—	—
Married	3,795	4,095	4,375	—	—	—	—
Wife's earned income							
allowance	2,425	2,605	2,785	—	—	—	—
Additional personal allowance	1,370	1,490	1,590	1,720	1,720	1,720	1,720
Income Tax Rates							
Lower rate						20%	20%
on first taxable						2,000	2,500
Basic rate	27%	25%	25%	25%	25%	25%	25%
on first taxable/on next	17,900	19,300	20,700	20,700	23,700	21,700	21,200
Higher rates	40%						
on next	2,500						
on next	45% 5,000						
on next	50% 7,900						
on next	55% 7,900						
and	60%	40%	40%	40%	40%	40%	40%
on excess over	41,200	19,300	20,700	20,700	23,700	23,700	23,700
Age allowances							
For age 65 to 74*							
Personal allowance	—	—	—	3,670	4,020	4,200	4,200
Married couple's allowance	—	—	—	2,145	2,355	2,465	2,465
Previous personal allowances							
Single	2,960	3,180	3,400	—	—	—	—
Married	4,675	5,035	5,385	—	—	—	—
For age 75 and over*							
Personal allowance	—	—	—	3,820	4,180	4,370	4,370
Married couple's allowance	—	—	—	2,185	2,395	2,505	2,505
Previous personal allowances							
Single	3,070	3,310	3,540	—	—	—	—
Married	4,845	5,205	5,565	—	—	—	—
Income limit	9,800	10,600	11,400	12,300	13,500	14,200	14,200

*For years up to and including 1988-89 increased age allowance available only from age 80: in 1989-90 and thereafter from age 75

Table 21 Capital Gains Tax Indexation Factors

To permit approximate calculation of the latent CGT relating to assets owned prior to March 1982 or acquired since that date

Year	Jan	Feb	Mar	Apr	May	Jun	Jul	Aug	Sep	Oct	Nov	Dec
82			1.754	1.719	1.707	1.702	1.701	1.701	1.702	1.693	1.685	1.688
83	1.686	1.679	1.676	1.653	1.646	1.642	1.633	1.626	1.619	1.613	1.607	1.603
84	1.604	1.597	1.592	1.572	1.566	1.562	1.563	1.549	1.546	1.536	1.532	1.533
85	1.527	1.515	1.501	1.470	1.463	1.460	1.463	1.459	1.460	1.457	1.458	1.450
86	1.447	1.442	1.440	1.426	1.424	1.424	1.428	1.424	1.417	1.415	1.403	1.398
87	1.393	1.387	1.385	1.368	1.367	1.367	1.368	1.364	1.360	1.354	1.347	1.348
88	1.348	1.343	1.338	1.317	1.312	1.307	1.306	1.291	1.285	1.272	1.266	1.263
89	1.255	1.246	1.240	1.219	1.211	1.207	1.206	1.203	1.195	1.186	1.176	1.173
90	1.166	1.159	1.147	1.113	1.103	1.099	1.098	1.087	1.077	1.069	1.072	1.072
91	1.069	1.064	1.060	1.046	1.043	1.038	1.041	1.039	1.035	1.031	1.027	1.027
92	1.027	1.022	1.019	1.004	1.000	1.000	1.004	1.003	1.000	1.000	1.000	1.001
93	1.010	1.004	1.000									

In **O'D v O'D** [1976] Fam 83 Ormrod LJ stated that capital gains tax on a notional disposal of the husband's assets should be taken into account 'to place the husband in approximately the right position on the scale of wealth'. This table enables this exercise to be performed without the use of the formula in the Retail Price Index table (Table 1).

It must be noted that this table is accurate for disposals (or notional disposals) in the month of March 1993, as the factors are calculated by reference to the RPI figure prevailing at that date. Hence as (or if) inflation progresses they will become slightly inaccurate.

Worked example for disposal (or notional disposal) in March 1993

The rules state that the indexation date is March 1982 or that of the month of acquisition, whichever is the later.

If a husband bought shares for £10,000 in March 1984, the indexation factor taken is 1.592. The uplifted base value is therefore £15,920.

If the shares are worth £50,000 in March 1993, then the taxable gain will be £34,080.

If the husband's annual exemption of £5,800 (for 1993-94) is already fully utilised, and his marginal rate of income tax is 40%, then the notional tax is £13,632, giving the shares a net value of £36,368.

Table 22 National Insurance Contributions

Class 1 Earnings Limits; and Class 2, Class 3 and Class 4 Limits and Contributions

		1992-93	1993-94
Class 1	Lower earnings limit	£54 p.w.	£56 p.w.
	Upper earnings limit	£405 p.w.	£420 p.w.
Class 2	Flat rate contribution	£5.35 p.w.	£5.55 p.w.
	Small earnings exception limit	£3,030 p.a.	£3,140 p.a.
Class 3	Flat rate contribution	£5.25 p.w.	£5.45 p.w.
Class 4	Lower profits limit	£6,120 p.a.	£6,340 p.a.
	Upper profits limit	£21,060 p.a.	£21,840 p.a.
	Contribution rate	6.3%	6.3%

Class 1 earnings limits apply only to employees' primary contributions.

Rates of Class 1 Contributions for 1993-94

Primary contribution (employee)		Secondary contribution (employer)		
Standard rate				
Not contracted-out rate %	**Contracted-out rate %**	**Weekly earnings**	**Not contracted-out rate %**	**Contracted-out rate %**
2% of £56 PLUS 9% of that part of earnings which exceeds £56 but does not exceed £420	2% of £56 PLUS 7.2% of that part of earnings which exceeds £56 but does not exceed £420	up to £56.00	4.6	4.6
		£56.00 to £94.99	4.6	1.6
		£95.00 to £139.99	6.6	3.6
		£140.00 to £194.99	8.6	5.6
		£195.00 to £420.00	10.4	7.4
		over £420.00	10.4	10.4

The reduced rate for married women and widow optants is 3.85% of earnings up to £420.00.

S/c contributions   88/89   4·05
                           89/90   4·25
                           90/91   4·55
                           91/92   5·15

Table 23   Social Security Benefits (Taxable)

Retirement Pension (non-means-tested)

	88-89	89-90	90-91	91-92	92-93	93-94	Total 93-94
Contributory							
Married couple							
both contributors — each	41.15	43.60	46.90	52.00	54.15	56.10	2,917.20
non-contributing spouse — extra	24.75	26.20	28.20	31.25	32.55	33.70	1,752.40
Single person	41.15	43.60	46.90	52.00	54.15	56.10	2,917.20
Non-contributory							
Married couple							
Category C	39.55	41.85	45.05	49.25	52.00	53.85	2,800.20
Category D	49.50	52.40	56.40	62.50	65.10	67.40	3,504.80
Single person	24.75	26.20	28.20	31.25	32.55	33.70	1,752.40

Amounts are per week, except for the far right-hand column, where the current annual rate is shown

Person over 80 years receives an additional £0.25 p.w. or £13 p.a.

Other Benefits

Category	92-93	93-94
Invalid Care Allowance (non-contributory; means-tested):	32.55	33.70
Spouse/person looking after child — extra	19.45	20.15
Statutory Maternity Pay (from employer; non-means-tested)		
Earning threshold	54.00	56.00
Lower rate	46.30	47.95
Statutory Sick Pay (from employer; non-means-tested)		
Earning threshold	54.00	56.00
Standard rate threshold	190.00	195.05
Standard rate	52.50	52.50
Lower rate	45.30	46.95
Unemployment Benefit (contributory; non-means-tested)		
Under pension age	43.10	44.65
Spouse/person looking after child — extra	26.60	27.55
Widow's Benefit (contributory; non-means-tested)		
Payment (lump sum; not taxable)	1,000.00	1,000.00
Widowed mother's allowance	54.15	56.10
Widow's pension (age-related) 45-54	16.25 to 50.36	16.83 to 52.17
55 or over	54.15	56.10

Amounts are per week, except for lump sum widow's benefit.

Table 24 Social Security Benefits (Non-taxable)

Category		92-93	93-94
Attendance Allowance (non-contributory; non-means-tested)			
Higher rate		43.35	44.90
Lower rate		28.95	30.00
Child Benefit (non-contributory; non-means-tested)			
Only/elder/eldest child		9.65	10.00
Each subsequent child		7.80	8.10
Council Tax Benefit Personal Allowances (income related; non-contributory)			
Single person	18-24		34.80
	25 or over		44.00
Lone parent	18 or over		44.00
Couple	One or both over 18		69.00
Dependent children	Under 11		15.05
	11-15		22.15
	16-17		26.45
	18		34.80
Disability Living Allowance (non-contributory; non-means-tested)			
Care component	Highest	43.35	44.90
	Middle	28.95	30.00
	Lower	11.55	11.95
Mobility component	Higher	30.30	31.40
	Lower	11.55	11.95
Disability Working Allowance (income related; non-contributory)			
Adult	Single person	42.40	43.95
	Couple/lone parent	58.80	60.95
Child	Under 11	10.40	10.75
	11–15	17.25	17.85
	16–17	21.45	22.20
	18 and over	29.90	31.00
Family Credit (income related; non-contributory)			
Adult credit		41.00	42.50
Child credit	Under 11	10.40	10.75
	11–15	17.25	17.85
	16–17	21.45	22.20
	18 and over	29.90	31.00
Guardian's Allowance (non-contributory; non-means-tested)		10.85	10.95

Amounts are per week

Table 24 Social Security Benefits (Non-taxable)

Category		92-93	93-94
Housing Benefit Personal Allowances (income related; non-contributory)			
Single person	16-24	33.60	34.80
	25 or over	42.45	44.00
Lone parent	Under 18	33.60	34.80
	18 or over	42.45	44.00
Couple	Both under 18	50.60	52.40
	One or both over 18	66.60	69.00
Dependent children	Under 11	14.55	15.05
	11-15	21.40	22.15
	16-17	25.55	26.45
	18	33.60	34.80
Invalidity Benefit (contributory; non-means-tested)*			
Pension		54.15	56.10
Spouse/person looking after child — extra		32.55	33.70
Invalidity allowancy	Higher rate	11.55	11.95
	Middle rate	7.20	7.50
	Lower rate	3.60	3.75
Maternity Allowance (contributory; non-means-tested)		42.25	43.75
Husband/person looking after child — extra		25.50	26.40
One Parent Benefit (non-contributory; non-means-tested)		5.85	6.05
Severe Disablement Allowance (non-contributory; non-means-tested)			
Basic rate		32.55	33.70
Spouse/person looking after child — extra		19.45	20.15
Age-related additions	Higher	11.55	11.95
	Middle	7.20	7.50
	Lower	3.60	3.75
Sickness Benefit (contributory; non-means-tested)*			
Over pension age		51.95	53.80
Spouse/person looking after child — extra		31.20	32.30
Under pension age		41.20	42.70
Spouse/person looking after child — extra		25.50	26.40
Social Fund (income related; non-contributory)			
Maternity payment		100.00	100.00

Amounts are per week, except for Social Fund payments which are lump sums.

*Unless as result of an industrial accident or disease.

Table 25 Income Support

Primary categories of Income Support

		92-93	93-94	Total 93-94
Personal Allowances				
Single person				
Under 18	Usual rate	25.55	26.45	1,375.40
	Higher rate	33.60	34.80	1,809.60
18-24		33.60	34.80	1,809.60
25 or over		42.45	44.00	2,288.00
Lone parent				
Under 18	Usual rate	25.55	26.45	1,375.40
	Higher rate	33.60	34.80	1,809.60
Over 18		42.45	44.00	2,288.00
Couple				
Both under 18		50.60	52.40	2,724.80
One or both over 18		66.60	69.00	3,588.00
Dependent children				
Under 11		14.55	15.05	782.60
11-15		21.40	22.15	1,151.80
16-17		25.55	26.45	1,375.40
18		33.60	34.80	1,809.60
Premiums				
Family		9.30	9.65	501.80
Lone parent		4.75	4.90	254.80
Disabled child		16.70	18.45	959.40
Carer		11.55	11.95	621.40
Pensioner	Single	16.70	17.30	899.60
	Couple	25.35	26.25	1,365.00
Pensioner Enhanced	Single	18.65	19.30	1,003.60
	Couple	28.00	29.00	1,508.00
Pensioner Higher	Single	22.75	23.55	1,224.60
	Couple	32.55	33.70	1,752.40
Disability	Single	17.80	18.45	959.40
	Couple	25.55	26.45	1,375.40
Severe Disability (per qualifying person)		32.55	33.70	1,752.40

Income Support benefits are means-tested; reduced if voluntarily unemployed, and then potentially taxable.

Amounts are per week, except for the far right-hand column, where the current annual rate is shown.

Table 26 Grossed-up Net Maintenance

The gross-income equivalent of maintenance, and some comparable salaries

Maintenance (£)	Grossed-up equivalent (£)	Comparable gross salaries
5,000	5,751	Student nurse (£6,920)
7,500	9,388	Army Private Class II (£9,997)
10,000	13,145	Teacher Grade III (£13,392)
12,500	16,797	Army Lieutenant (£16,667)
15,000	20,456	Ward Sister Class I (£20,350)
17,500	24,152	Head Teacher Point 10 (£25,710)
20,000	27,824	Major after 1 year (£26,744)
22,500	32,367	M.P. (£30,854); Major after 8 years (£32,051)
25,000	36,664	Dentist (£36,352)
27,500	40,963	Lieutenant Colonel (£37,518); G.P. (£40,610)
30,000	45,266	Parliamentary Under-Secretary (£44,611)
		Colonel after 4 years (£44,848)
32,500	49,492	Head Teacher Point 50 (£49,848)
		Minister of State (£51,402)
35,000	53,842	Brigadier (£53,600); District Judge at PRFD (£56,035)
37,500	58,126	Leader of the Opposition (£59,736)
40,000	62,438	Secretary of State (£63,047)
42,500	66,682	Circuit Judge (£65,912)
45,000	71,050	Judge Advocate-General (£69,412)
47,500	75,355	Prime Minister (£76,234)
50,000	79,591	Second Permanent Secretary (Civil Service) (£80,600)
52,500	83,950	
55,000	88,245	High Court Judge (£90,148)
57,500	92,469	
60,000	96,816	Lord Justice of Appeal (£99,510)
62,500	101,098	Permanent Secretary to the Treasury (£101,920)
65,000	105,408	Lord of Appeal, and Master of the Rolls (£103,800)
67,500	109,649	Secretary to the Cabinet (£108,940)
70,000	114,013	Lord Chief Justice (£112,083)
		Lord Chancellor (£114,083)

Sources: *Whitaker's Almanack,* Lord Chancellor's Department, *Daily Telegraph*

Assumptions for the grossed-up equivalent: 1993-94 tax rates; 3% contributory pension; contracted out of Class 1 NIC. Terms and conditions for the comparable gross salaries are various.

Table 27   Big Money Awards

This table analyses awards made to the wife in seven notable reported big money clean break cases

Initial award

Case	Assets (£)	Award (£)	Proportion (%)	Years of marriage
O'D (1974)	215,000	70,000	32.6	12
Page (1980)	388,137	120,000	30.9	41
Preston (1980)	2,350,000	700,000	29.8	23
Duxbury (1984)	2,700,000	750,000	27.8	22
Newton (1988)	2,500,000	750,000	30.0	18
E v E* (1989)	1,500,000	450,000	30.0	16
Gojkovic** (1989)	4,000,000	1,295,000	32.4	17

Award per year of marriage (adjusted for inflation)

Case	Adjusted assets (£)	Adjusted award (£)	Award per year of marriage (£)	Years of marriage
O'D (1974)	748,699	243,736	20,314	12
Page (1980)	710,717	219,732	5,359	41
Preston (1980)	3,957,804	1,178,920	51,257	23
Duxbury (1984)	3,657,466	1,015,963	46,180	22
Newton (1988)	2,718,849	815,655	45,314	18
E v E* (1989)	1,631,309	489,393	30,587	16
Gojkovic** (1989)	4,350,158	1,408,364	82,845	17

The table demonstrates a uniformity of approach as to the conventional proportion awarded, but reveals inconsistencies in attributing weight to the length of the marriage.

It must be remembered that the exercise is essentially one of discretion, and thus this table should not be taken too seriously.

For full citations see subheading 'Money, big' under **Leading Cases**.

*Over half the award was in trust
**Seventeen years of marriage included nine years premarital cohabitation

Perpetual calendar

The number opposite each of the years in the list below indicates which of the calendars on the following pages is the one for that year. Thus the number opposite 1999 is 6, so calendar 6 can be used as a 1999 calendar.

Leap years

Years divisible by four without remainder are leap years with 366 days instead of 365 (29 days in February instead of 28). However the last year of a century is not a leap year except when divisible by 400.

Easter Sunday

These dates will apply, unless there is a change to a fixed Easter

1980	6 April	1987	19 April	1994	3 April
1981	19 April	1988	3 April	1995	16 April
1982	11 April	1989	26 March	1996	7 April
1983	3 April	1990	15 April	1997	30 March
1984	22 April	1991	31 March	1998	12 April
1985	7 April	1992	19 April	1999	4 April
1986	30 March	1993	11 April	2000	23 April

Year	Calendar	Year	Calendar	Year	Calendar	Year	Calendar	Year	Calendar	Year	Calendar
1901	3	1926	6	1951	2	1976	12	2001	2	2026	5
1902	4	1927	7	1952	10	1977	7	2002	3	2027	6
1903	5	1928	8	1953	5	1978	1	2003	4	2028	14
1904	13	1929	3	1954	6	1979	2	2004	12	2029	2
1905	1	1930	4	1955	7	1980	10	2005	7	2030	3
1906	2	1931	5	1956	8	1981	5	2006	1	2031	4
1907	3	1932	13	1957	3	1982	6	2007	2	2032	12
1908	11	1933	1	1958	4	1983	7	2008	10	2033	7
1909	6	1934	2	1959	5	1984	8	2009	5	2034	1
1910	7	1935	3	1960	13	1985	3	2010	6	2035	2
1911	1	1936	11	1961	1	1986	4	2011	7	2036	10
1912	9	1937	6	1962	2	1987	5	2012	8	2037	5
1913	4	1938	7	1963	3	1988	13	2013	3	2038	6
1914	5	1939	1	1964	11	1989	1	2014	4	2039	7
1915	6	1940	9	1965	6	1990	2	2015	5	2040	8
1916	14	1941	4	1966	7	1991	3	2016	13	2041	3
1917	2	1942	5	1967	1	1992	11	2017	1	2042	4
1918	3	1943	6	1968	9	1993	6	2018	2	2043	5
1919	4	1944	14	1969	4	1994	7	2019	3	2044	13
1920	12	1945	2	1970	5	1995	1	2020	11	2045	1
1921	7	1946	3	1971	6	1996	9	2021	6	2046	2
1922	1	1947	4	1972	14	1997	4	2022	7	2047	3
1923	2	1948	12	1973	2	1998	5	2023	1	2048	11
1924	10	1949	7	1974	3	1999	6	2024	9	2049	6
1925	5	1950	1	1975	4	2000	14	2025	4	2050	7

1

January
```
M     2  9 16 23 30
T     3 10 17 24 31
W     4 11 18 25
T     5 12 19 26
F     6 13 20 27
S     7 14 21 28
S   1 8 15 22 29
```
February
```
      6 13 20 27
      7 14 21 28
    1 8 15 22
    2 9 16 23
  3 10 17 24
  4 11 18 25
  5 12 19 26
```
March
```
      6 13 20 27
      7 14 21 28
    1 8 15 22 29
    2 9 16 23 30
  3 10 17 24 31
  4 11 18 25
  5 12 19 26
```
April
```
      3 10 17 24
      4 11 18 25
      5 12 19 26
      6 13 20 27
      7 14 21 28
    1 8 15 22 29
    2 9 16 23 30
```
May
```
M   1 8 15 22 29
T   2 9 16 23 30
W   3 10 17 24 31
T   4 11 18 25
F   5 12 19 26
S   6 13 20 27
S   7 14 21 28
```
June
```
      5 12 19 26
      6 13 20 27
      7 14 21 28
    1 8 15 22 29
    2 9 16 23 30
  3 10 17 24
  4 11 18 25
```
July
```
      3 10 17 24 31
      4 11 18 25
      5 12 19 26
      6 13 20 27
      7 14 21 28
    1 8 15 22 29
    2 9 16 23 30
```
August
```
      7 14 21 28
    1 8 15 22 29
    2 9 16 23 30
    3 10 17 24 31
    4 11 18 25
    5 12 19 26
    6 13 20 27
```
September
```
M     4 11 18 25
T     5 12 19 26
W     6 13 20 27
T     7 14 21 28
F   1 8 15 22 29
S   2 9 16 23 30
S   3 10 17 24
```
October
```
      2 9 16 23 30
      3 10 17 24 31
      4 11 18 25
      5 12 19 26
      6 13 20 27
      7 14 21 28
    1 8 15 22 29
```
November
```
      6 13 20 27
      7 14 21 28
    1 8 15 22 29
    2 9 16 23 30
    3 10 17 24
    4 11 18 25
    5 12 19 26
```
December
```
      4 11 18 25
      5 12 19 26
      6 13 20 27
      7 14 21 28
    1 8 15 22 29
    2 9 16 23 30
    3 10 17 24 31
```

2

January
```
M   1 8 15 22 29
T   2 9 16 23 30
W   3 10 17 24 31
T   4 11 18 25
F   5 12 19 26
S   6 13 20 27
S   7 14 21 28
```
February
```
      5 12 19 26
      6 13 20 27
      7 14 21 28
    1 8 15 22
    2 9 16 23
  3 10 17 24
  4 11 18 25
```
March
```
      5 12 19 26
      6 13 20 27
      7 14 21 28
    1 8 15 22 29
    2 9 16 23 30
  3 10 17 24 31
  4 11 18 25
```
April
```
      2 9 16 23 30
      3 10 17 24
      4 11 18 25
      5 12 19 26
      6 13 20 27
      7 14 21 28
    1 8 15 22 29
```
May
```
M     7 14 21 28
T   1 8 15 22 29
W   2 9 16 23 30
T   3 10 17 24 31
F   4 11 18 25
S   5 12 19 26
S   6 13 20 27
```
June
```
      4 11 18 25
      5 12 19 26
      6 13 20 27
      7 14 21 28
    1 8 15 22 29
    2 9 16 23 30
  3 10 17 24
```
July
```
      2 9 16 23 30
      3 10 17 24 31
      4 11 18 25
      5 12 19 26
      6 13 20 27
      7 14 21 28
    1 8 15 22 29
```
August
```
      6 13 20 27
      7 14 21 28
    1 8 15 22 29
    2 9 16 23 30
    3 10 17 24 31
    4 11 18 25
    5 12 19 26
```
September
```
M     3 10 17 24
T     4 11 18 25
W     5 12 19 26
T     6 13 20 27
F     7 14 21 28
S   1 8 15 22 29
S   2 9 16 23 30
```
October
```
    1 8 15 22 29
    2 9 16 23 30
    3 10 17 24 31
    4 11 18 25
    5 12 19 26
    6 13 20 27
    7 14 21 28
```
November
```
      5 12 19 26
      6 13 20 27
      7 14 21 28
    1 8 15 22 29
    2 9 16 23 30
    3 10 17 24
    4 11 18 25
```
December
```
      3 10 17 24 31
      4 11 18 25
      5 12 19 26
      6 13 20 27
      7 14 21 28
    1 8 15 22 29
    2 9 16 23 30
```

Perpetual calendar

3

January
M 7 14 21 28
T 1 8 15 22 29
W 2 9 16 23 30
T 3 10 17 24 31
F 4 11 18 25
S 5 12 19 26
S 6 13 20 27

February
M 4 11 18 25
T 5 12 19 26
W 6 13 20 27
T 7 14 21 28
F 1 8 15 22
S 2 9 16 23
S 3 10 17 24

March
M 4 11 18 25
T 5 12 19 26
W 6 13 20 27
T 7 14 21 28
F 1 8 15 22 29
S 2 9 16 23 30
S 3 10 17 24 31

April
M 1 8 15 22 29
T 2 9 16 23 30
W 3 10 17 24
T 4 11 18 25
F 5 12 19 26
S 6 13 20 27
S 7 14 21 28

May
M 6 13 20 27
T 7 14 21 28
W 1 8 15 22 29
T 2 9 16 23 30
F 3 10 17 24 31
S 4 11 18 25
S 5 12 19 26

June
M 3 10 17 24
T 4 11 18 25
W 5 12 19 26
T 6 13 20 27
F 7 14 21 28
S 1 8 15 22 29
S 2 9 16 23 30

July
M 1 8 15 22 29
T 2 9 16 23 30
W 3 10 17 24 31
T 4 11 18 25
F 5 12 19 26
S 6 13 20 27
S 7 14 21 28

August
M 5 12 19 26
T 6 13 20 27
W 7 14 21 28
T 1 8 15 22 29
F 2 9 16 23 30
S 3 10 17 24 31
S 4 11 18 25

September
M 2 9 16 23 30
T 3 10 17 24
W 4 11 18 25
T 5 12 19 26
F 6 13 20 27
S 7 14 21 28
S 1 8 15 22 29

October
M 7 14 21 28
T 1 8 15 22 29
W 2 9 16 23 30
T 3 10 17 24 31
F 4 11 18 25
S 5 12 19 26
S 6 13 20 27

November
M 4 11 18 25
T 5 12 19 26
W 6 13 20 27
T 7 14 21 28
F 1 8 15 22 29
S 2 9 16 23 30
S 3 10 17 24

December
M 2 9 16 23 30
T 3 10 17 24 31
W 4 11 18 25
T 5 12 19 26
F 6 13 20 27
S 7 14 21 28
S 1 8 15 22 29

4

January
M 6 13 20 27
T 7 14 21 28
W 1 8 15 22 29
T 2 9 16 23 30
F 3 10 17 24 31
S 4 11 18 25
S 5 12 19 26

February
M 3 10 17 24
T 4 11 18 25
W 5 12 19 26
T 6 13 20 27
F 7 14 21 28
S 1 8 15 22
S 2 9 16 23

March
M 3 10 17 24 31
T 4 11 18 25
W 5 12 19 26
T 6 13 20 27
F 7 14 21 28
S 1 8 15 22 29
S 2 9 16 23 30

April
M 7 14 21 28
T 1 8 15 22 29
W 2 9 16 23 30
T 3 10 17 24
F 4 11 18 25
S 5 12 19 26
S 6 13 20 27

May
M 5 12 19 26
T 6 13 20 27
W 7 14 21 28
T 1 8 15 22 29
F 2 9 16 23 30
S 3 10 17 24 31
S 4 11 18 25

June
M 2 9 16 23 30
T 3 10 17 24
W 4 11 18 25
T 5 12 19 26
F 6 13 20 27
S 7 14 21 28
S 1 8 15 22 29

July
M 7 14 21 28
T 1 8 15 22 29
W 2 9 16 23 30
T 3 10 17 24 31
F 4 11 18 25
S 5 12 19 26
S 6 13 20 27

August
M 4 11 18 25
T 5 12 19 26
W 6 13 20 27
T 7 14 21 28
F 1 8 15 22 29
S 2 9 16 23 30
S 3 10 17 24 31

September
M 1 8 15 22 29
T 2 9 16 23 30
W 3 10 17 24
T 4 11 18 25
F 5 12 19 26
S 6 13 20 27
S 7 14 21 28

October
M 6 13 20 27
T 7 14 21 28
W 1 8 15 22 29
T 2 9 16 23 30
F 3 10 17 24 31
S 4 11 18 25
S 5 12 19 26

November
M 3 10 17 24
T 4 11 18 25
W 5 12 19 26
T 6 13 20 27
F 7 14 21 28
S 1 8 15 22 29
S 2 9 16 23 30

December
M 1 8 15 22 29
T 2 9 16 23 30
W 3 10 17 24 31
T 4 11 18 25
F 5 12 19 26
S 6 13 20 27
S 7 14 21 28

5

January
M 5 12 19 26
T 6 13 20 27
W 7 14 21 28
T 1 8 15 22 29
F 2 9 16 23 30
S 3 10 17 24 31
S 4 11 18 25

February
M 2 9 16 23
T 3 10 17 24
W 4 11 18 25
T 5 12 19 26
F 6 13 20 27
S 7 14 21 28
S 1 8 15 22

March
M 2 9 16 23 30
T 3 10 17 24 31
W 4 11 18 25
T 5 12 19 26
F 6 13 20 27
S 7 14 21 28
S 1 8 15 22 29

April
M 6 13 20 27
T 7 14 21 28
W 1 8 15 22 29
T 2 9 16 23 30
F 3 10 17 24
S 4 11 18 25
S 5 12 19 26

May
M 4 11 18 25
T 5 12 19 26
W 6 13 20 27
T 7 14 21 28
F 1 8 15 22 29
S 2 9 16 23 30
S 3 10 17 24 31

June
M 1 8 15 22 29
T 2 9 16 23 30
W 3 10 17 24
T 4 11 18 25
F 5 12 19 26
S 6 13 20 27
S 7 14 21 28

July
M 6 13 20 27
T 7 14 21 28
W 1 8 15 22 29
T 2 9 16 23 30
F 3 10 17 24 31
S 4 11 18 25
S 5 12 19 26

August
M 3 10 17 24 31
T 4 11 18 25
W 5 12 19 26
T 6 13 20 27
F 7 14 21 28
S 1 8 15 22 29
S 2 9 16 23 30

September
M 7 14 21 28
T 1 8 15 22 29
W 2 9 16 23 30
T 3 10 17 24
F 4 11 18 25
S 5 12 19 26
S 6 13 20 27

October
M 5 12 19 26
T 6 13 20 27
W 7 14 21 28
T 1 8 15 22 29
F 2 9 16 23 30
S 3 10 17 24 31
S 4 11 18 25

November
M 2 9 16 23 30
T 3 10 17 24
W 4 11 18 25
T 5 12 19 26
F 6 13 20 27
S 7 14 21 28
S 1 8 15 22 29

December
M 7 14 21 28
T 1 8 15 22 29
W 2 9 16 23 30
T 3 10 17 24 31
F 4 11 18 25
S 5 12 19 26
S 6 13 20 27

6

January
M 4 11 18 25
T 5 12 19 26
W 6 13 20 27
T 7 14 21 28
F 1 8 15 22 29
S 2 9 16 23 30
S 3 10 17 24 31

February
M 1 8 15 22
T 2 9 16 23
W 3 10 17 24
T 4 11 18 25
F 5 12 19 26
S 6 13 20 27
S 7 14 21 28

March
M 1 8 15 22 29
T 2 9 16 23 30
W 3 10 17 24 31
T 4 11 18 25
F 5 12 19 26
S 6 13 20 27
S 7 14 21 28

April
M 5 12 19 26
T 6 13 20 27
W 7 14 21 28
T 1 8 15 22 29
F 2 9 16 23 30
S 3 10 17 24
S 4 11 18 25

May
M 3 10 17 24 31
T 4 11 18 25
W 5 12 19 26
T 6 13 20 27
F 7 14 21 28
S 1 8 15 22 29
S 2 9 16 23 30

June
M 7 14 21 28
T 1 8 15 22 29
W 2 9 16 23 30
T 3 10 17 24
F 4 11 18 25
S 5 12 19 26
S 6 13 20 27

July
M 5 12 19 26
T 6 13 20 27
W 7 14 21 28
T 1 8 15 22 29
F 2 9 16 23 30
S 3 10 17 24 31
S 4 11 18 25

August
M 2 9 16 23 30
T 3 10 17 24 31
W 4 11 18 25
T 5 12 19 26
F 6 13 20 27
S 7 14 21 28
S 1 8 15 22 29

September
M 6 13 20 27
T 7 14 21 28
W 1 8 15 22 29
T 2 9 16 23 30
F 3 10 17 24
S 4 11 18 25
S 5 12 19 26

October
M 4 11 18 25
T 5 12 19 26
W 6 13 20 27
T 7 14 21 28
F 1 8 15 22 29
S 2 9 16 23 30
S 3 10 17 24 31

November
M 1 8 15 22 29
T 2 9 16 23 30
W 3 10 17 24
T 4 11 18 25
F 5 12 19 26
S 6 13 20 27
S 7 14 21 28

December
M 6 13 20 27
T 7 14 21 28
W 1 8 15 22 29
T 2 9 16 23 30
F 3 10 17 24 31
S 4 11 18 25
S 5 12 19 26

7

January
M 3 10 17 24 31
T 4 11 18 25
W 5 12 19 26
T 6 13 20 27
F 7 14 21 28
S 1 8 15 22 29
S 2 9 16 23 30

February
M 7 14 21 28
T 1 8 15 22
W 2 9 16 23
T 3 10 17 24
F 4 11 18 25
S 5 12 19 26
S 6 13 20 27

March
M 7 14 21 28
T 1 8 15 22 29
W 2 9 16 23 30
T 3 10 17 24 31
F 4 11 18 25
S 5 12 19 26
S 6 13 20 27

April
M 4 11 18 25
T 5 12 19 26
W 6 13 20 27
T 7 14 21 28
F 1 8 15 22 29
S 2 9 16 23 30
S 3 10 17 24

May
M 2 9 16 23 30
T 3 10 17 24 31
W 4 11 18 25
T 5 12 19 26
F 6 13 20 27
S 7 14 21 28
S 1 8 15 22 29

June
M 6 13 20 27
T 7 14 21 28
W 1 8 15 22 29
T 2 9 16 23 30
F 3 10 17 24
S 4 11 18 25
S 5 12 19 26

July
M 4 11 18 25
T 5 12 19 26
W 6 13 20 27
T 7 14 21 28
F 1 8 15 22 29
S 2 9 16 23 30
S 3 10 17 24 31

August
M 1 8 15 22 29
T 2 9 16 23 30
W 3 10 17 24 31
T 4 11 18 25
F 5 12 19 26
S 6 13 20 27
S 7 14 21 28

September
M 5 12 19 26
T 6 13 20 27
W 7 14 21 28
T 1 8 15 22 29
F 2 9 16 23 30
S 3 10 17 24
S 4 11 18 25

October
M 3 10 17 24 31
T 4 11 18 25
W 5 12 19 26
T 6 13 20 27
F 7 14 21 28
S 1 8 15 22 29
S 2 9 16 23 30

November
M 7 14 21 28
T 1 8 15 22 29
W 2 9 16 23 30
T 3 10 17 24
F 4 11 18 25
S 5 12 19 26
S 6 13 20 27

December
M 5 12 19 26
T 6 13 20 27
W 7 14 21 28
T 1 8 15 22 29
F 2 9 16 23 30
S 3 10 17 24 31
S 4 11 18 25

8

January
M 2 9 16 23 30
T 3 10 17 24 31
W 4 11 18 25
T 5 12 19 26
F 6 13 20 27
S 7 14 21 28
S 1 8 15 22 29

February
M 6 13 20 27
T 7 14 21 28
W 1 8 15 22 29
T 2 9 16 23
F 3 10 17 24
S 4 11 18 25
S 5 12 19 26

March
M 5 12 19 26
T 6 13 20 27
W 7 14 21 28
T 1 8 15 22 29
F 2 9 16 23 30
S 3 10 17 24 31
S 4 11 18 25

April
M 2 9 16 23 30
T 3 10 17 24
W 4 11 18 25
T 5 12 19 26
F 6 13 20 27
S 7 14 21 28
S 1 8 15 22 29

May
M 7 14 21 28
T 1 8 15 22 29
W 2 9 16 23 30
T 3 10 17 24 31
F 4 11 18 25
S 5 12 19 26
S 6 13 20 27

June
M 4 11 18 25
T 5 12 19 26
W 6 13 20 27
T 7 14 21 28
F 1 8 15 22 29
S 2 9 16 23 30
S 3 10 17 24

July
M 2 9 16 23 30
T 3 10 17 24 31
W 4 11 18 25
T 5 12 19 26
F 6 13 20 27
S 7 14 21 28
S 1 8 15 22 29

August
M 6 13 20 27
T 7 14 21 28
W 1 8 15 22 29
T 2 9 16 23 30
F 3 10 17 24 31
S 4 11 18 25
S 5 12 19 26

September
M 3 10 17 24
T 4 11 18 25
W 5 12 19 26
T 6 13 20 27
F 7 14 21 28
S 1 8 15 22 29
S 2 9 16 23 30

October
M 1 8 15 22 29
T 2 9 16 23 30
W 3 10 17 24 31
T 4 11 18 25
F 5 12 19 26
S 6 13 20 27
S 7 14 21 28

November
M 5 12 19 26
T 6 13 20 27
W 7 14 21 28
T 1 8 15 22 29
F 2 9 16 23 30
S 3 10 17 24
S 4 11 18 25

December
M 3 10 17 24 31
T 4 11 18 25
W 5 12 19 26
T 6 13 20 27
F 7 14 21 28
S 1 8 15 22 29
S 2 9 16 23 30

Perpetual calendar

9

January
```
M  1   8  15  22  29
T  2   9  16  23  30
W  3  10  17  24  31
T  4  11  18  25
F  5  12  19  26
S  6  13  20  27
S  7  14  21  28
```

February
```
M  5  12  19  26
T  6  13  20  27
W  7  14  21  28
T  1   8  15  22  29
F  2   9  16  23
S  3  10  17  24
S  4  11  18  25
```

March
```
M  4  11  18  25
T  5  12  19  26
W  6  13  20  27
T  7  14  21  28
F  1   8  15  22  29
S  2   9  16  23  30
S  3  10  17  24  31
```

April
```
M  1   8  15  22  29
T  2   9  16  23  30
W  3  10  17  24
T  4  11  18  25
F  5  12  19  26
S  6  13  20  27
S  7  14  21  28
```

May
```
M  6  13  20  27
T  7  14  21  28
W  1   8  15  22  29
T  2   9  16  23  30
F  3  10  17  24  31
S  4  11  18  25
S  5  12  19  26
```

June
```
M  3  10  17  24
T  4  11  18  25
W  5  12  19  26
T  6  13  20  27
F  7  14  21  28
S  1   8  15  22  29
S  2   9  16  23  30
```

July
```
M  1   8  15  22  29
T  2   9  16  23  30
W  3  10  17  24  31
T  4  11  18  25
F  5  12  19  26
S  6  13  20  27
S  7  14  21  28
```

August
```
M  5  12  19  26
T  6  13  20  27
W  7  14  21  28
T  1   8  15  22  29
F  2   9  16  23  30
S  3  10  17  24  31
S  4  11  18  25
```

September
```
M  2   9  16  23  30
T  3  10  17  24
W  4  11  18  25
T  5  12  19  26
F  6  13  20  27
S  7  14  21  28
S  1   8  15  22  29
```

October
```
M  7  14  21  28
T  1   8  15  22  29
W  2   9  16  23  30
T  3  10  17  24  31
F  4  11  18  25
S  5  12  19  26
S  6  13  20  27
```

November
```
M  4  11  18  25
T  5  12  19  26
W  6  13  20  27
T  7  14  21  28
F  1   8  15  22  29
S  2   9  16  23  30
S  3  10  17  24
```

December
```
M  2   9  16  23  30
T  3  10  17  24  31
W  4  11  18  25
T  5  12  19  26
F  6  13  20  27
S  7  14  21  28
S  1   8  15  22  29
```

10

January
```
M  7  14  21  28
T  1   8  15  22  29
W  2   9  16  23  30
T  3  10  17  24  31
F  4  11  18  25
S  5  12  19  26
S  6  13  20  27
```

February
```
M  4  11  18  25
T  5  12  19  26
W  6  13  20  27
T  7  14  21  28
F  1   8  15  22  29
S  2   9  16  23
S  3  10  17  24
```

March
```
M  3  10  17  24  31
T  4  11  18  25
W  5  12  19  26
T  6  13  20  27
F  7  14  21  28
S  1   8  15  22  29
S  2   9  16  23  30
```

April
```
M  7  14  21  28
T  1   8  15  22  29
W  2   9  16  23  30
T  3  10  17  24
F  4  11  18  25
S  5  12  19  26
S  6  13  20  27
```

May
```
M  5  12  19  26
T  6  13  20  27
W  7  14  21  28
T  1   8  15  22  29
F  2   9  16  23  30
S  3  10  17  24  31
S  4  11  18  25
```

June
```
M  2   9  16  23  30
T  3  10  17  24
W  4  11  18  25
T  5  12  19  26
F  6  13  20  27
S  7  14  21  28
S  1   8  15  22  29
```

July
```
M  7  14  21  28
T  1   8  15  22  29
W  2   9  16  23  30
T  3  10  17  24  31
F  4  11  18  25
S  5  12  19  26
S  6  13  20  27
```

August
```
M  4  11  18  25
T  5  12  19  26
W  6  13  20  27
T  7  14  21  28
F  1   8  15  22  29
S  2   9  16  23  30
S  3  10  17  24  31
```

September
```
M  1   8  15  22  29
T  2   9  16  23  30
W  3  10  17  24
T  4  11  18  25
F  5  12  19  26
S  6  13  20  27
S  7  14  21  28
```

October
```
M  6  13  20  27
T  7  14  21  28
W  1   8  15  22  29
T  2   9  16  23  30
F  3  10  17  24  31
S  4  11  18  25
S  5  12  19  26
```

November
```
M  3  10  17  24
T  4  11  18  25
W  5  12  19  26
T  6  13  20  27
F  7  14  21  28
S  1   8  15  22  29
S  2   9  16  23  30
```

December
```
M  1   8  15  22  29
T  2   9  16  23  30
W  3  10  17  24  31
T  4  11  18  25
F  5  12  19  26
S  6  13  20  27
S  7  14  21  28
```

11

January
```
M  6  13  20  27
T  7  14  21  28
W  1   8  15  22  29
T  2   9  16  23  30
F  3  10  17  24  31
S  4  11  18  25
S  5  12  19  26
```

February
```
M  3  10  17  24
T  4  11  18  25
W  5  12  19  26
T  6  13  20  27
F  7  14  21  28
S  1   8  15  22  29
S  2   9  16  23
```

March
```
M  2   9  16  23  30
T  3  10  17  24  31
W  4  11  18  25
T  5  12  19  26
F  6  13  20  27
S  7  14  21  28
S  1   8  15  22  29
```

April
```
M  6  13  20  27
T  7  14  21  28
W  1   8  15  22  29
T  2   9  16  23  30
F  3  10  17  24
S  4  11  18  25
S  5  12  19  26
```

May
```
M  4  11  18  25
T  5  12  19  26
W  6  13  20  27
T  7  14  21  28
F  1   8  15  22  29
S  2   9  16  23  30
S  3  10  17  24  31
```

June
```
M  1   8  15  22  29
T  2   9  16  23  30
W  3  10  17  24
T  4  11  18  25
F  5  12  19  26
S  6  13  20  27
S  7  14  21  28
```

July
```
M  6  13  20  27
T  7  14  21  28
W  1   8  15  22  29
T  2   9  16  23  30
F  3  10  17  24  31
S  4  11  18  25
S  5  12  19  26
```

August
```
M  3  10  17  24  31
T  4  11  18  25
W  5  12  19  26
T  6  13  20  27
F  7  14  21  28
S  1   8  15  22  29
S  2   9  16  23  30
```

September
```
M  7  14  21  28
T  1   8  15  22  29
W  2   9  16  23  30
T  3  10  17  24
F  4  11  18  25
S  5  12  19  26
S  6  13  20  27
```

October
```
M  5  12  19  26
T  6  13  20  27
W  7  14  21  28
T  1   8  15  22  29
F  2   9  16  23  30
S  3  10  17  24  31
S  4  11  18  25
```

November
```
M  2   9  16  23  30
T  3  10  17  24
W  4  11  18  25
T  5  12  19  26
F  6  13  20  27
S  7  14  21  28
S  1   8  15  22  29
```

December
```
M  7  14  21  28
T  1   8  15  22  29
W  2   9  16  23  30
T  3  10  17  24  31
F  4  11  18  25
S  5  12  19  26
S  6  13  20  27
```

12

January
```
M  5  12  19  26
T  6  13  20  27
W  7  14  21  28
T  1   8  15  22  29
F  2   9  16  23  30
S  3  10  17  24  31
S  4  11  18  25
```

February
```
M  2   9  16  23
T  3  10  17  24
W  4  11  18  25
T  5  12  19  26
F  6  13  20  27
S  7  14  21  28
S  1   8  15  22  29
```

March
```
M  1   8  15  22  29
T  2   9  16  23  30
W  3  10  17  24  31
T  4  11  18  25
F  5  12  19  26
S  6  13  20  27
S  7  14  21  28
```

April
```
M  5  12  19  26
T  6  13  20  27
W  7  14  21  28
T  1   8  15  22  29
F  2   9  16  23  30
S  3  10  17  24
S  4  11  18  25
```

May
```
M  3  10  17  24  31
T  4  11  18  25
W  5  12  19  26
T  6  13  20  27
F  7  14  21  28
S  1   8  15  22  29
S  2   9  16  23  30
```

June
```
M  7  14  21  28
T  1   8  15  22  29
W  2   9  16  23  30
T  3  10  17  24
F  4  11  18  25
S  5  12  19  26
S  6  13  20  27
```

July
```
M  5  12  19  26
T  6  13  20  27
W  7  14  21  28
T  1   8  15  22  29
F  2   9  16  23  30
S  3  10  17  24  31
S  4  11  18  25
```

August
```
M  2   9  16  23  30
T  3  10  17  24  31
W  4  11  18  25
T  5  12  19  26
F  6  13  20  27
S  7  14  21  28
S  1   8  15  22  29
```

September
```
M  6  13  20  27
T  7  14  21  28
W  1   8  15  22  29
T  2   9  16  23  30
F  3  10  17  24
S  4  11  18  25
S  5  12  19  26
```

October
```
M  4  11  18  25
T  5  12  19  26
W  6  13  20  27
T  7  14  21  28
F  1   8  15  22  29
S  2   9  16  23  30
S  3  10  17  24  31
```

November
```
M  1   8  15  22  29
T  2   9  16  23  30
W  3  10  17  24
T  4  11  18  25
F  5  12  19  26
S  6  13  20  27
S  7  14  21  28
```

December
```
M  6  13  20  27
T  7  14  21  28
W  1   8  15  22  29
T  2   9  16  23  30
F  3  10  17  24  31
S  4  11  18  25
S  5  12  19  26
```

13

January
```
M  4  11  18  25
T  5  12  19  26
W  6  13  20  27
T  7  14  21  28
F  1   8  15  22  29
S  2   9  16  23  30
S  3  10  17  24  31
```

February
```
M  1   8  15  22  29
T  2   9  16  23
W  3  10  17  24
T  4  11  18  25
F  5  12  19  26
S  6  13  20  27
S  7  14  21  28
```

March
```
M  7  14  21  28
T  1   8  15  22  29
W  2   9  16  23  30
T  3  10  17  24  31
F  4  11  18  25
S  5  12  19  26
S  6  13  20  27
```

April
```
M  4  11  18  25
T  5  12  19  26
W  6  13  20  27
T  7  14  21  28
F  1   8  15  22  29
S  2   9  16  23  30
S  3  10  17  24
```

May
```
M  2   9  16  23  30
T  3  10  17  24  31
W  4  11  18  25
T  5  12  19  26
F  6  13  20  27
S  7  14  21  28
S  1   8  15  22  29
```

June
```
M  6  13  20  27
T  7  14  21  28
W  1   8  15  22  29
T  2   9  16  23  30
F  3  10  17  24
S  4  11  18  25
S  5  12  19  26
```

July
```
M  4  11  18  25
T  5  12  19  26
W  6  13  20  27
T  7  14  21  28
F  1   8  15  22  29
S  2   9  16  23  30
S  3  10  17  24  31
```

August
```
M  1   8  15  22  29
T  2   9  16  23  30
W  3  10  17  24  31
T  4  11  18  25
F  5  12  19  26
S  6  13  20  27
S  7  14  21  28
```

September
```
M  5  12  19  26
T  6  13  20  27
W  7  14  21  28
T  1   8  15  22  29
F  2   9  16  23  30
S  3  10  17  24
S  4  11  18  25
```

October
```
M  3  10  17  24  31
T  4  11  18  25
W  5  12  19  26
T  6  13  20  27
F  7  14  21  28
S  1   8  15  22  29
S  2   9  16  23  30
```

November
```
M  7  14  21  28
T  1   8  15  22  29
W  2   9  16  23  30
T  3  10  17  24
F  4  11  18  25
S  5  12  19  26
S  6  13  20  27
```

December
```
M  5  12  19  26
T  6  13  20  27
W  7  14  21  28
T  1   8  15  22  29
F  2   9  16  23  30
S  3  10  17  24  31
S  4  11  18  25
```

14

January
```
M  3  10  17  24  31
T  4  11  18  25
W  5  12  19  26
T  6  13  20  27
F  7  14  21  28
S  1   8  15  22  29
S  2   9  16  23  30
```

February
```
M  7  14  21  28
T  1   8  15  22  29
W  2   9  16  23
T  3  10  17  24
F  4  11  18  25
S  5  12  19  26
S  6  13  20  27
```

March
```
M  6  13  20  27
T  7  14  21  28
W  1   8  15  22  29
T  2   9  16  23  30
F  3  10  17  24  31
S  4  11  18  25
S  5  12  19  26
```

April
```
M  3  10  17  24
T  4  11  18  25
W  5  12  19  26
T  6  13  20  27
F  7  14  21  28
S  1   8  15  22  29
S  2   9  16  23  30
```

May
```
M  1   8  15  22  29
T  2   9  16  23  30
W  3  10  17  24  31
T  4  11  18  25
F  5  12  19  26
S  6  13  20  27
S  7  14  21  28
```

June
```
M  5  12  19  26
T  6  13  20  27
W  7  14  21  28
T  1   8  15  22  29
F  2   9  16  23  30
S  3  10  17  24
S  4  11  18  25
```

July
```
M  3  10  17  24  31
T  4  11  18  25
W  5  12  19  26
T  6  13  20  27
F  7  14  21  28
S  1   8  15  22  29
S  2   9  16  23  30
```

August
```
M  7  14  21  28
T  1   8  15  22  29
W  2   9  16  23  30
T  3  10  17  24  31
F  4  11  18  25
S  5  12  19  26
S  6  13  20  27
```

September
```
M  4  11  18  25
T  5  12  19  26
W  6  13  20  27
T  7  14  21  28
F  1   8  15  22  29
S  2   9  16  23  30
S  3  10  17  24
```

October
```
M  2   9  16  23  30
T  3  10  17  24  31
W  4  11  18  25
T  5  12  19  26
F  6  13  20  27
S  7  14  21  28
S  1   8  15  22  29
```

November
```
M  6  13  20  27
T  7  14  21  28
W  1   8  15  22  29
T  2   9  16  23  30
F  3  10  17  24
S  4  11  18  25
S  5  12  19  26
```

December
```
M  4  11  18  25
T  5  12  19  26
W  6  13  20  27
T  7  14  21  28
F  1   8  15  22  29
S  2   9  16  23  30
S  3  10  17  24  31
```

Leading Cases

We believe the following list of cases (arranged chronologically under each subject heading) represents the leading cases on each topic. Inevitably it is a subjective selection and no doubt readers will feel that we have omitted relevant cases or included irrelevant ones. For example, in particular areas we have mentioned only a few major cases out of a substantial total. Similarly, the legal aid cases selected are those where the legal aid charge bears on the ancillary relief result, rather than the many cases where the court has considered whether the charge is or is not applicable.

Adjournment of claims

Morgan v Morgan	[1977] Fam 122, [1977] 2 All ER 515, [1977] 2 WLR 712
Morris v Morris	(1977) 7 Fam Law 244, CA
Priest v Priest	[1980] 1 FLR 189, CA
Milne v Milne	[1981] FLR 286, CA
Hardy v Hardy	[1981] FLR 321, CA
Davies v Davies	[1986] 1 FLR 497, CA
Roberts v Roberts	[1986] 2 All ER 483, [1986] 1 WLR 437, [1986] 2 FLR 152
Michael v Michael	[1986] 2 FLR 389, CA
Ranson v Ranson	[1988] 1 WLR 183, [1988] 1 FLR 292, CA
MT v MT (financial provision: lump sum)	[1992] 1 FLR 362

Agreements

Hyman v Hyman	[1929] AC 601, [1929] All ER Rep 245, HL
Backhouse v Backhouse	[1978] 1 All ER 1158, [1978] 1 WLR 243
Dean v Dean	[1978] Fam 161, [1978] 3 All ER 758, [1978] 3 WLR 288
Edgar v Edgar	[1980] 3 All ER 887, [1980] 1 WLR 1410, CA
Camm v Camm	[1983] 4 FLR 577, CA
Simister v Simister (No. 2)	[1987] 1 FLR 194
Amey v Amey	[1992] 2 FLR 89

Appealing out of time

Johnson v Johnson	[1980] FLR 331, CA
Warren v Warren	[1983] 4 FLR 529, CA
Barder v Barder (Caluori intervening)	[1988] AC 20, [1987] 2 All ER 440, [1987] 2 WLR 1350, HL
Rooker v Rooker	[1988] 1 FLR 219, CA
Hope-Smith v Hope-Smith	[1989] 2 FLR 56, CA
Edmonds v Edmonds	[1990] 2 FLR 202, CA
Smith v Smith	[1992] Fam 69, [1991] 2 All ER 306, [1991] 3 WLR 646, CA
Thompson v Thompson	[1991] 2 FLR 530, CA
Wells v Wells	[1992] 2 FLR 66, CA
Chaudhuri v Chaudhuri	[1992] 2 FLR 73, CA
Barber v Barber	[1993] 1 FLR 476, CA

Appeals

Ladd v Marshall	[1954] 3 All ER 745, [1954] 1 WLR 1489, CA
G (formerly P) v P (ancillary relief: appeal)	[1978] 1 All ER 1099, [1977] 1 WLR 1376, CA
Marsh v Marsh	[1993] 1 FLR 467, CA

Arrears

Fowler v Fowler	[1981] FLR 141, CA
Russell v Russell	[1986] 1 FLR 465, CA
Bernstein v O'Neill	[1989] 2 FLR 1

Children (capital provision)

Chamberlain v Chamberlain	[1974] 1 All ER 33, [1973] 1 WLR 1557, CA
Lilford (Lord) v Glyn	[1979] 1 All ER 441, [1979] 1 WLR 78, CA
Griffiths v Griffiths	[1984] Fam 70, [1984] 2 All ER 626, [1984] 3 WLR 165, CA

Leading Cases

Children (capital provision) (Cont'd)
Kiely v Kiely   [1988] 1 FLR 248, CA
K v K   [1992] 2 All ER 727, [1992] 1 WLR 530, [1992] 2 FLR 220, CA

Children (non-marital, income provision)
Haroutunian v Jennings·   [1980] 1 FLR 62, Div Ct
Osborn v Sparks   [1982] 3 FLR 90, Div Ct

Clean break/termination
Hanlon v Hanlon   [1978] 2 All ER 889, [1978] 1 WLR 592, CA
Pearce v Pearce   [1980] 1 FLR 261, CA
Morris v Morris   [1985] FLR 1176, CA
Seaton v Seaton   [1986] 2 FLR 398, CA
S v S   [1986] Fam 189, [1986] 3 All ER 566, [1986] 3 WLR 518;
                                 on appeal [1987] 2 All ER 312, [1987] 1 WLR 382n, CA
M v M   [1987] 2 FLR 1
Suter v Suter & Jones   [1987] Fam 111, [1987] 2 All ER 336, [1987] 3 WLR 9, CA
Whiting v Whiting   [1988] 2 All ER 275, [1988] 1 WLR 565, [1988] 2 FLR 189, CA
Barrett v Barrett   [1988] 2 FLR 516
C v C   [1989] 1 FLR 11
Hepburn v Hepburn   [1989] 1 FLR 373, CA
Waterman v Waterman   [1989] 1 FLR 380, CA
Fisher v Fisher   [1989] 1 FLR 423, CA
Clutton v Clutton   [1991] 1 All ER 340, [1991] 1 WLR 359, [1991] 1 FLR 242, CA

Companies
Potter v Potter   [1982] 3 All ER 321, [1982] 1 WLR 1255, [1983] 4 FLR 331, CA
Smith v Smith   [1983] 4 FLR 154, CA
Re Bird Precision Bellows   [1984] Ch 419, [1984] 3 All ER 444, [1984] 2 WLR 869
Nicholas v Nicholas   [1984] FLR 285, CA
Buckingham v Francis   [1986] 2 All ER 738
Bullock v Bullock   [1986] 1 FLR 372, CA
B v B   [1989] 1 FLR 119
P v P   [1989] 2 FLR 241
Evans v Evans   [1990] 2 All ER 147, [1990] 1 FLR 319

Conduct
Sexual
Brett v Brett   [1969] 1 All ER 1007, [1969] 1 WLR 487, CA
Harnett v Harnett   [1973] Fam 156, [1973] 2 All ER 593, [1973] 3 WLR 1;
                                 affd [1974] 1 All ER 764, [1974] 1 WLR 219, CA
Cuzner v Underdown   [1974] 2 All ER 351, [1974] 1 WLR 641, CA
Bailey v Tolliday   [1983] FLR 542

Violence, etc
Jones v Jones   [1976] Fam 8, [1975] 2 All ER 12, [1975] 2 WLR 606, CA
M v M (financial provision:
   conduct)   [1982] FLR 83
Kyte v Kyte   [1988] Fam 145, [1987] 3 All ER 1041, [1987] 3 WLR 1114, CA
Evans v Evans   [1989] 1 FLR 351, CA

Financial misconduct
Martin v Martin   [1976] Fam 335, [1976] 3 All ER 625, [1976] 3 WLR 580, CA
Primavera v Primavera   [1992] 1 FLR 16, CA

Misconduct of proceedings
B v B (real property: assessment
   of interests)   [1988] 2 FLR 490

Leading Cases

Conduct (Cont'd)
Other

Robinson v Robinson	[1981] FLR 1, CA
Robinson v Robinson	[1983] Fam 42, [1983] 1 All ER 391, [1983] 2 WLR 146, CA
Vasey v Vasey	[1985] FLR 596, CA
K v K (conduct)	[1990] 2 FLR 225

Costs
Inter partes

Calderbank v Calderbank	[1976] Fam 93, [1975] 3 All ER 333, [1975] 3 WLR 586, CA
Cutts v Head	[1984] Ch 290, [1984] 1 All ER 597, [1984] 2 WLR 349, CA
Moorish v Moorish	[1984] Fam Law 26, CA
Singer v Sharegin	[1984] FLR 114, CA
Atkinson v Atkinson	[1984] FLR 524, CA
Leary v Leary	[1987] 1 All ER 261, [1987] 1 WLR 72, [1987] 1 FLR 384, CA
S v S	[1989] FCR 570
E v E	[1990] 2 FLR 233
Gojkovic v Gojkovic (No.2)	[1992] Fam 40, [1992] 1 All ER 267, [1991] 3 WLR 621, CA
In re Elgindata Ltd (No.2)	[1992] 1 WLR 1207, CA

Orders against legal advisers

Myers v Elman	[1939] 4 All ER 484, [1940] AC 282, HL
Davy-Chiesman v Davy-Chiesman	[1985] Fam 48, [1984] 1 All ER 321, [1984] 2 WLR 291, CA
Sinclair-Jones v Kay	[1988] 2 All ER 611, [1989] 1 WLR 114, CA
Gupta v Comer	[1991] 2 WLR 494, CA
Chrulew v Borm-Reid & Co	[1992] 1 All ER 953, [1992] 1 WLR 176
Re a Barrister (wasted costs order) (No. 1 of 1991)	[1992] 3 All ER 610

Delay

Lombardi v Lombardi	[1973] 3 All ER 625, [1973] 1 WLR 1276, CA
Chaterjee v Chaterjee	[1976] Fam 199, [1976] 1 All ER 719, [1976] 2 WLR 397, CA
Chambers v Chambers	[1980] 1 FLR 10
Fraser v Fraser	[1982] 3 FLR 98, CA
D v W	(1984) 14 Fam Law 152
Twiname v Twiname	[1992] 1 FLR 29, CA

Division by one-third

Wachtel v Wachtel	[1973] Fam 72, [1973] 1 All ER 829, [1973] 2 WLR 366, CA
Sibley v Sibley	[1981] 2 FLR 121
Furniss v Furniss	[1982] 3 FLR 46, CA

Farms

P v P	[1978] 3 All ER 70, [1978] 1 WLR 483, CA
S v S	(1980) 10 Fam Law 240

Inheritance (Provision for Family and Dependants) Act

Re Coventry, Coventry v Coventry	[1980] Ch 461, [1979] 3 All ER 815, [1979] 3 WLR 802, CA
Re Besterman (deceased)	[1984] Ch 458, [1984] 2 All ER 656, [1984] 3 WLR 280, CA
Bishop v Plumley	[1991] 1 All ER 236, [1991] 1 WLR 582, [1991] 1 FLR 121, CA
Moody v Stevenson	[1992] Ch 486, [1992] 2 All ER 524, [1992] 2 WLR 640
Jessop v Jessop	[1992] 1 FLR 591

Leading Cases

Interim capital orders/orders for sale

Crosthwaite v Crosthwaite	[1989] 2 FLR 86, CA
Barry v Barry	[1992] Fam 140, [1992] 3 All ER 405, [1992] 2 WLR 799
Green v Green	[1993] 1 FLR 326

Joint names

Browne v Pritchard	[1975] 3 All ER 721, [1975] 1 WLR 1366, CA
Walsh v Corcoran	[1983] 4 FLR 59, CA

Legal aid

Effect on order

Collins v Collins	[1987] 1 FLR 226, CA
Scallon v Scallon	[1990] 1 FLR 194, CA

Incidence of charge

Till v Till	[1974] 1 QB 558, [1974] 1 All ER 1096, [1974] 2 WLR 447, CA
Hanlon v Law Society	[1981] AC 124, [1980] 2 All ER 199, [1980] 2 WLR 756, HL
Draskovic v Draskovic	(1981) 11 Fam Law 87
Manley v Law Society	[1981] 1 All ER 401, [1981] 1 WLR 335, CA
Van Hoorn v Law Society	[1985] QB 106, [1984] 3 All ER 136, [1984] 3 WLR 199
Curling v Law Society	[1985] 1 All ER 705, [1985] 1 WLR 470, [1985] FLR 831, CA
Watkinson v Legal Aid Board	[1991] 2 All ER 953, [1991] 1 WLR 419, [1991] 2 FLR 26, CA

Length of marriage: cohabitation before

Campbell v Campbell	[1976] Fam 347, [1977] 1 All ER 1, [1976] 3 WLR 572
Kokosinski v Kokosinski	[1980] Fam 72, [1980] 1 All ER 1106, [1980] 3 WLR 55
Foley v Foley	[1981] Fam 160, [1981] 2 All ER 857, [1981] 3 WLR 284, CA

Length of marriage, short

S v S	[1977] Fam 127, [1977] 1 All ER 56, [1977] 3 WLR 775, CA
Churchill v Churchill	(1981) 11 Fam Law 179, CA
H v H	[1981] 2 FLR 392
Robertson v Robertson	[1983] 4 FLR 387
H (formerly W) v H	(1983) 13 Fam Law 180
Attar v Attar (No.2)	[1985] FLR 653
Hedges v Hedges	[1991] 1 FLR 196, CA

Mareva and section 37 injunctions

Jordan v Jordan	(1965) Sol Jo 353
Smith v Smith	(1973) 3 Fam Law 80
Mareva Cia Naviera SA v International Bulkcarriers SA	[1980] 1 All ER 213, CA
Roche v Roche	(1981) 11 Fam Law 243, CA
Hamlin v Hamlin	[1986] Fam 11, [1985] 2 All ER 1037, [1985] 3 WLR 629, CA
Kemmis v Kemmis	[1988] 1 WLR 1307, [1988] 2 FLR 223, CA
Lloyds Bowmaker Ltd v Britannia Arrow Holdings plc	[1988] 3 All ER 178, [1988] 1 WLR 1337, CA
Brink's-MAT Ltd v Elcombe	[1988] 3 All ER 188, [1988] 1 WLR 1350, CA
Babanaft International Co SA v Bassatne	[1990] Ch 13, [1989] 1 All ER 433, [1989] 2 WLR 232, CA
Derby & Co Ltd v Weldon (No.1)	[1989] 1 All ER 469, [1989] 2 WLR 276, CA
Derby & Co Ltd v Weldon (No.2)	[1989] 1 All ER 1002, CA
Derby & Co Ltd v Weldon (No.6)	[1990] 3 All ER 263, [1990] 1 WLR 1189, CA
Crittenden v Crittenden	[1990] 2 FLR 361, CA
Shipman v Shipman	[1991] 1 FLR 250
Sherry v Sherry	[1991] 1 FLR 307, CA
Ghoth v Ghoth	[1992] 2 All ER 920, [1992] 2 FLR 300, CA

Leading Cases

Money, big

O'D v O'D	[1976] Fam 83, [1975] 2 All ER 993, [1975] 3 WLR 308, CA
Preston v Preston	[1982] Fam 17, [1982] 1 All ER 41, [1982] 3 WLR 619, CA
Re Besterman (deceased)	[1984] Ch 458, [1984] 2 All ER 656, [1984] 3 WLR 280, CA
Attar v Attar (No. 1)	[1985] FLR 649
S v S	[1986] Fam 189, [1986] 3 All ER 566, [1986] 3 WLR 518;
	on appeal [1987] 2 All ER 312, [1987] 1 WLR 382n, CA
Duxbury v Duxbury	[1992] Fam 62n, [1990] 2 All ER 77, [1991] 3 WLR 639, CA
Boylan v Boylan	[1988] 1 FLR 282
Newton v Newton	[1990] 1 FLR 33, CA
Gojkovic v Gojkovic	[1992] Fam 40, [1990] 2 All ER 84, [1991] 3WLR 621, CA
B v B (financial provision: discovery)	[1990] 2 FLR 180
E v E	[1990] 2 FLR 233
Vicary v Vicary	[1992] 2 FLR 271, CA

Money, small

Barnes v Barnes	[1972] 3 All ER 872, [1972] 1 WLR 1381, CA
Peacock v Peacock	[1984] 1 All ER 1069, [1984] 1 WLR 532, [1984] FLR 263
Freeman v Swatridge	[1984] FLR 762, CA
Ashley v Blackman	[1988] Fam 85, [1988] 3WLR 222, [1988] 2 FLR 278
Delaney v Delaney	[1990] 2 FLR 457, CA

Net effect

Furniss v Furniss	[1982] 3 FLR 46, CA
Stockford v Stockford	[1982] 3 FLR 58, CA
Slater v Slater & Another	[1982] 3 FLR 364, CA
Titheradge v Titheradge	[1983] 4 FLR 552, CA
Allen v Allen	[1986] 2 FLR 265, CA

Non-disclosure/discovery

J v J	[1955] P 215, [1955] 3 WLR 72, [1955] 2 All ER 617, CA
Weisz v Weisz	(1975) Times 16 December, CA
Robinson v Robinson	[1982] 2 All ER 699, [1982] 1 WLR 786, [1983] 4 FLR 102
Desai v Desai	(1982) 13 Fam Law 46
Livesey v Jenkins	[1985] AC 424, [1985] 1 All ER 106, [1985] 2 WLR 47, HL
B-T v B-T	[1990] 2 FLR 1
E v E	[1990] 2 FLR 233
G v G	[1992] 1 FLR 40
Hildebrand v Hildebrand	[1992] 1 FLR 244

Orders on property

Mesher v Mesher & Hall	[1980] 1 All ER 126n, CA
Martin v Martin	[1978] Fam 12, [1977] 3 All ER 762, [1977] 3 WLR 101, CA
Dunford v Dunford	[1980] 1 All ER 122, [1980] 1 WLR 5, CA
Harvey v Harvey	[1982] Fam 83, [1982] 1 All ER 693, [1982] 2 WLR 283, CA
Mortimer v Mortimer-Griffin	[1986] 2 FLR 315, CA
Clutton v Clutton	[1991] 1 All ER 340, [1991] 1 WLR 359, [1991] 1 FLR 242, CA
Popat v Popat	[1991] 2 FLR 163, CA

Parity of assets

Page v Page	[1981] 2 FLR 198
Schuller v Schuller	[1990] 2 FLR 193, CA

Leading Cases

Pensions
Edmonds v Edmonds   [1965] 1 All ER 379n, [1965] 1 WLR 58
Le Marchant v Le Marchant   [1977] 3 All ER 610, [1977] 1 WLR 559, CA
Richardson v Richardson   (1979) 9 Fam Law 86, CA
Priest v Priest   [1980] 1 FLR 189, CA
Walker v Walker   [1983] Fam 68, [1983] 2 All ER 909, [1983] 3 WLR 421, CA
Roberts v Roberts   [1986] 2 All ER 483, [1986] 1 WLR 437, [1986] 2 FLR 152
Ranson v Ranson   [1988] 1 WLR 183, [1988] 1 FLR 292, CA
Happé v Happé   [1991] 4 All ER 527, [1990] 1 WLR 1282, [1990] 2 FLR 212, CA
Hedges v Hedges   [1991] 1 FLR 196, CA
Cotgrave v Cotgrave   [1992] Fam 33, [1991] 4 All ER 537, [1991] 3 WLR 567, CA

Property, beneficial interest in
Sole name
Pettitt v Pettitt   [1970] AC 777, [1969] 2 All ER 385, [1969] 2 WLR 966, HL
Gissing v Gissing   [1971] AC 886, [1970] 2 All ER 780, [1970] 3 WLR 255, HL
Grant v Edwards   [1986] Ch 638, [1986] 2 All ER 426, [1986] 3 WLR 114, CA
Lloyds Bank v Rosset   [1991] 1 AC 107, [1990] 1 All ER 1111, [1990] 2 WLR 867, HL
Risch v McFee   [1991] 1 FLR 105, CA
Stokes v Anderson   [1991] 1 FLR 391
Hammond v Mitchell   [1991] 1 WLR 1127; sub nom H v M [1992] 1 FLR 229

Joint names
Bernard v Josephs   [1982] Ch 391, [1982] 3 All ER 162, [1982] 2 WLR 1052, CA
Goodman v Gallant   [1986] Fam 106, [1986] 1 All ER 311, [1986] 2 WLR 236, CA
Marsh v von Sternberg   [1986] 1 FLR 526
Springette v Defoe   [1992] 2 FLR 388, CA

Remarriage and cohabitation
Prospects
Wachtel v Wachtel   [1973] Fam 72, [1973] 1 All ER 829, [1973] 2 WLR 366, CA
S v S   [1976] Fam 18n, [1975] 2 WLR 615n; sub nom Smith v Smith,
                                 [1975] 2 All ER 19n
Livesey v Jenkins   [1985] AC 424, [1985] 1 All ER 106, [1985] 2 WLR 47, HL

Actual remarriage
H v H   [1975] Fam 9, [1975] 1 All ER 367, [1975] 2 WLR 124
Prow (formerly Brown) v Brown   [1982] FLR 352, CA
Stockford v Stockford   [1982] FLR 58, CA
Camm v Camm   [1983] FLR 577, CA

Cohabitation
Blower v Blower   [1986] 1 FLR 292
Suter v Suter and Jones   [1987] Fam 111, [1987] 2 All ER 336, [1987] 3 WLR 9, CA
Atkinson v Atkinson   [1988] Fam 93, [1987] 3 All ER 849, [1988] 2 WLR 204, CA
R v R   [1988] 1 FLR 89, CA
Hepburn v Hepburn   [1989] 1 FLR 373, CA
Duxbury v Duxbury   [1992] Fam 62n, [1990] 2 All ER 77, [1991] 3 WLR 639, CA

Resources, extent of
Lombardi v Lombardi   [1973] 3 All ER 625, [1973] 1 WLR 1276, CA
Armstrong v Armstrong   (1974) 4 Fam Law 156, CA
Daubney v Daubney   [1976] Fam 267, [1976] 2 All ER 453, [1976] 2 WLR 959, CA
P v P (financial provision)   [1978] 3 All ER 70, [1978] 1 WLR 483, CA
Pearce v Pearce   [1980] FLR 261, CA
Schuller v Schuller   [1990] 2 FLR 193, CA
Wagstaff v Wagstaff   [1992] 1 All ER 275, [1992] 1 WLR 320, [1992] 1 FLR 333, CA

Leading Cases

Second wife/cohabitee, means of

Roberts v Roberts	[1970] P 1, [1968] 3 All ER 479, [1968] 3 WLR 1181, Div Ct
Macey v Macey	[1982] 3 FLR 7
Slater v Slater & Another	[1982] 3 FLR 364, CA
Suter v Suter & Jones	[1987] Fam 111, [1987] 2 All ER 336, [1987] 3 WLR 9, CA
Atkinson v Atkinson	[1988] Fam 93, [1987] 3 All ER 849, [1988] 2 WLR 204, CA

Trusts

Howard v Howard	[1945] P 1, [1945] 1 All ER 91, CA
Re Londonderry's Settlement	[1965] Ch 918, [1964] 3 All ER 855, [1965] 2 WLR 229, CA
B v B	[1982] 3 FLR 298, CA
Browne v Browne	[1989] 1 FLR 291, CA
E v E	[1990] 2 FLR 233

Variation of final orders

Carson v Carson	[1983] 1 All ER 478, [1983] 1 WLR 285, [1981] 2 FLR 352, CA
Sandford v Sandford	[1986] 1 FLR 412, CA
Thompson v Thompson	[1986] Fam 38, [1985] 2 All ER 243, [1985] 3 WLR 17, CA
Dinch v Dinch	[1987] 1 All ER 818, [1987] 1 WLR 252, [1987] 2 FLR 162, HL
Peacock v Peacock	[1991] 1 FLR 324
Popat v Popat	[1991] 2 FLR 163, CA

Variation of periodical payments orders

Primavera v Primavera	[1992] 1 FLR 16, CA
Garner v Garner	[1992] 1 FLR 573, CA

Matrimonial Causes Act 1973

25. Matters to which court is to have regard in deciding how to exercise its powers under ss. 23, 24 and 24A.

(1) It shall be the duty of the court in deciding whether to exercise its powers under section 23, 24 or 24A above and, if so, in what manner, to have regard to all the circumstances of the case, first consideration being given to the welfare while a minor of any child of the family who has not attained the age of eighteen.

(2) As regards the exercise of the powers of the court under section 23 (1) (a), (b) or (c), 24 or 24A above in relation to a party to the marriage, the court shall in particular have regard to the following matters –

(a) the income, earning capacity, property and other financial resources which each of the parties to the marriage has or is likely to have in the forseeable future, including in the case of earning capacity any increase in that capacity which it would in the opinion of the court be reasonable to expect a party to the marriage to take steps to acquire;

(b) the financial needs, obligations and responsibilities which each of the parties to the marriage has or is likely to have in the foreseeable future;

(c) the standard of living enjoyed by the family before the breakdown of the marriage;

(d) the age of each party to the marriage and the duration of the marriage;

(e) any physical or mental disability of either of the parties to the marriage;

(f) the contributions which each of the parties has made or is likely in the foreseeable future to make to the welfare of the family, including any contribution by looking after the home or caring for the family;

(g) the conduct of each of the parties, if that conduct is such that it would in the opinion of the court be inequitable to disregard it;

(h) in the case of proceedings for divorce or nullity of marriage, the value to each of the parties to the marriage of any benefit (for example, a pension) which, by reason of the dissolution or annulment of the marriage, that party will lose the chance of acquiring.

(3) As regards the exercise of the powers of the court under section 23 (1) (d), (e) or (f), (2) or (4), 24 or 24A above in relation to a child of the family, the court shall in particular have regard to the following matters –

(a) the financial needs of the child;

(b) the income, earning capacity (if any), property and other financial resources of the child;

(c) any physical or mental disability of the child;

(d) the manner in which he was being and in which the parties to the marriage expected him to be educated or trained;

(e) the considerations mentioned in relation to the parties to the marriage in paragraphs (a), (b), (c) and (e) of subsection (2) above.

(4) As regards the exercise of the powers of the court under section 23 (1) (d), (e) or (f), (2) or (4), 24 or 24A above against a party to a marriage in favour of a child of the family who is not the child of that party, the court shall also have regard –

(a) to whether that party assumed any responsibility for the child's maintenance, and, if so, to the extent to which, and the basis upon which, that party assumed such responsibility and to the length of time for which that party discharged such responsibility;

(b) to whether in assuming and discharging such responsibility that party did so knowing that the child was not his or her own;

(c) to the liability of any other person to maintain the child.

25A. Exercise of court's powers in favour of party to marriage on decree of divorce or nullity of marriage.

(1) Where on or after the grant of a decree of divorce or nullity of marriage the court decides to exercise its powers under section 23 (1) (a), (b) or (c), 24 or 24A above in favour of a party to the marriage, it shall be the duty of the court to consider whether it would be appropriate so to exercise those powers that the financial obligations of each party towards the other will be terminated as soon after the grant of the decree as the court considers just and reasonable.

(2) Where the court decides in such a case to make a periodical payments or secured periodical payments order in favour of a party to the marriage, the court shall in particular consider whether it would be appropriate to require those payments to be made or secured only for such term as would in the opinion of the court be sufficient to enable the party in whose favour the order is made to adjust without undue hardship to the termination of his or her financial dependence on the other party.

(3) Where on or after the grant of a decree of divorce or nullity of marriage an application is made by a party to the marriage for a periodical payments or secured periodical payments order in his or her favour, then, if the court considers that no continuing obligation should be imposed on either party to make or secure periodical payments in favour of the other, the court may dismiss the application with a direction that the applicant shall not be entitled to make any further application in relation to that marriage for an order under section 23 (1) (a) or (b) above.

Matrimonial Causes Act 1973

31. Variation, discharge, etc. of certain orders for financial relief.

(1) Where the court has made an order to which this section applies, then, subject to the provisions of this section and of section 28 (1A) above, the court shall have power to vary or discharge the order or to suspend any provision thereof temporarily and to revive the operation of any provision so suspended.

(2) This section applies to the following orders, that is to say –

(a) any order for maintenance pending suit and any interim order for maintenance;

(b) any periodical payments order;

(c) any secured periodical payments order;

(d) any order made by virtue of section 23 (3) (c) or 27 (7) (b) above (provision for payment of a lump sum by instalments);

(e) any order for a settlement of property under section 24 (1) (b) or for a variation of settlement under section 24 (1) (c) or (d) above, being an order made on or after the grant of a decree of judicial separation;

(f) any order made under section 24A (1) above for the sale of property.

(2A) Where the court has made an order referred to in subsection (2) (a), (b) or (c) above, then subject to the provisions of this section, the court shall have power to remit the payment of any arrears due under the order or of any part thereof.

(3) The powers exercisable by the court under this section in relation to an order shall be exercisable also in relation to any instrument executed in pursuance of the order.

(4) The court shall not exercise the powers conferred by this section in relation to an order for a settlement under section 24 (1) (b) or for a variation of settlement under section 24 (1) (c) or (d) above except on an application made in proceedings –

(a) for the rescission of the decree of judicial separation by reference to which the order was made, or

(b) for the dissolution of the marriage in question.

(5) No property adjustment order shall be made on an application for the variation of a periodical payments or secured periodical payments order made (whether in favour of a party to a marriage or in favour of a child of the family) under section 23 above, and no order for the payment of a lump sum shall be made on an application for the variation of a periodical payments or secured periodical payments order in favour of a party to a marriage (whether made under section 23 or under section 27 above).

(6) Where the person liable to make payments under a secured periodical payments order has died, an application under this section relating to that order (and to any order made under section 24A (1) above which requires the proceeds of sale of property to be used for securing those payments) may be made by the person entitled to payments under the periodical payments order or by the personal representatives of the deceased person, but no such application shall, except with the permission of the court, be made after the end of the period of six months from the date on which representation in regard to the estate of that person is first taken out.

(7) In exercising the powers conferred by this section the court shall have regard to all the circumstances of the case, first consideration being given to the welfare while a minor of any child of the family who has not attained the age of eighteen, and the circumstances of the case shall include any change in any of the matters to which the court was required to have regard when making the order to which the application relates, and –

(a) in the case of a periodical payments or secured periodical payments order made on or after the grant of a decree of divorce or nullity of marriage, the court shall consider whether in all the circumstances and after having regard to any such change it would be appropriate to vary the order so that payments under the order are required to be made or secured only for such further period as will in the opinion of the court be sufficient to enable the party in whose favour the order was made to adjust without undue hardship to the termination of those payments;

(b) in a case where the party against whom the order was made has died, the circumstances of the case shall also include the changed circumstances resulting from his or her death.

(8) The personal representatives of a deceased person against whom a secured periodical payments order was made shall not be liable for having distributed any part of the estate of the deceased after the expiration of the period of six months referred to in subsection (6) above on the ground that they ought to have taken into account the possibility that the court might permit an application under this section to be made after that period by the person entitled to payments under the order; but this subsection shall not prejudice any power to recover any part of the estate so distributed arising by virtue of the making of an order in pursuance of this section.

(9) In considering for the purposes of subsection (6) above the question when representation was first taken out, a grant limited to settled land or to trust property shall be left out of account and a grant limited to real estate or to personal estate shall be left out of account unless a grant limited to the remainder of the estate has previously been made or is made at the same time.

(10) Where the court, in exercise of its powers under this section, decides to vary or discharge a periodical payments or secured periodical payments order, then, subject to section 28 (1) and (2) above, the court shall have power to direct that the variation or discharge shall not take effect until the expiration of such period as may be specified in the order.